REMEMBER ME

BENEDICT OLAGUNJU

MINISTRY IN ART PUBLISHING

Ministry In Art Publishing Ltd
e-mail: info@miapublishing.com
www.miapublishing.com

Unless otherwise stated, all scripture quotations are taken from the Holy
Bible, New Living Translation (NLT). Other versions cited are NIV, NKJV,
AMP and KJV. Quotations marked NIV are taken from the HOLY BIBLE,
NEW INTERNATIONAL VERSION. Copyright © 1973, 1978, 1984 by
International Bible Society. Used by permission of Hodder and Stoughton
Ltd, a member of the Hodder Headline Plc Group. All rights reserved.
"NIV" is a registered trademark of International Bible Society.
UK trademark number 1448790.

Quotations marked KJV are from the Holy Bible,
King James Version.

ISBN: 978-1-907402-10-4

Cover design: Allan Sealy

Contents

❧

Acknowledgements

Great praise must go to my Great God, the Almighty Jehovah, the giver of all good gifts, who made inspiration and desire available for writing this book.

I appreciate you my wife Benedicta, the Bible says, 'he who finds a wife finds a good thing' (Proverbs 18: 22) and this is my testimony. You often abandoned your personal pursuits to pursue the completion of this book. Surely the honour and blessings of a wife who covers her husband's nakedness and enhances his gifting will rest upon you abundantly. Thank you for who you are; you have all my love Darling.

I treasure you all dear children; Maria, Benedict, Michael, Deborah and my granddaughter Johanna, for your relentless support and understanding at all times. Pen and paper cannot fully express my love and appreciation for you.

My very warm gratitude goes to Rev. George Adegboye my dear father and mentor. May your coast always be enlarged, you have taught me many Godly values and I thank you for taking the time to write the foreword of this book in the midst of your extremely busy schedule.

A special thanks to Rev. Dr. Goodluck Christopher. I thank you for your love and support, your encouragement motivates and propels me in the right direction.

Sincere appreciation to my God chosen Father in the Lord Pastor Stephen Olanrewaju, a man God used to bring me from obscurity to light You are truly my Barnabas sir.

Elder, Dr Remi Folorunsho you are a rare gem. Your advice, patience and wisdom shared are invaluable. I thank God for your heart of openness to share deep things with me that has helped the writing of this book.

To my boys divinely called 'The Kingsforce': Deacon Olalekan Bello a man of undiluted faithfulness and submission, Bro Seyi Kolawole a man of unbroken focus, Bro Fidelis Ukwenu a man committed to excellence and Bro Michael Sangoranti a man of transparent personality. I appreciate the pains you bore and the sacrifices made by you all. But for you Fidelis, your interest in the success of this book is so great that anything less than perfection would not satisfy you as you proofread, edited, corrected and typed the manuscripts as you would in any other academic thesis.

Last but not least, I appreciate all the members of Focus International Christian Centre (FICC). You are a wonderful congregation, thanks for being there for me.

❦

Endorsement

Finite beings are prone to forget, but the infinite God does not forget His people. Pharaoh's cup bearer forgot Joseph, but God remembered him. He is constantly reminding us that He will not forget His children. Can a woman forget her suckling child, that she should not have compassion on the son of her womb? Yea, they may forget, yet will not I forget thee. (Isaiah 49:15) Again, He re-assures us: Remember these, O Jacob and Israel; for thou art my Servant; I have formed thee; thou art my servant: O Israel, thou shalt not be forgotten of me. (Isaiah 44:21). Moreover, God has "graven" us "upon the palms of His hands" (Isaiah 49:16) and we are "the apple of His eyes" (Psalm 17:8; Zech. 2:8). Therefore, you cannot be forgotten.

Our God is the God of remembrance. He has never, and will never forget His children. It is inconsistent with His nature to forget promises or covenants. Indeed, He is "not unrighteous to forget" our labours and expectations (Heb. 6:10). As the Omnipotent God, He knows all things and remembers every detail minutely, about your life and destiny.

God "remembers us in our low estates" (Psalm 136:23). He remembers you when you are sick, tired, discouraged and lonely. Even when you are old and weak, the Lord will not forget you (Isa. 46:4). Divine remembrance is synonymous with Divine visitation or divine intervention. It brings Divine blessings or Heavenly bounties, uncommon miracles, Divine favour, miraculous answers to prayers, solutions to seemingly hopeless and impossible conditions, inexplicable breakthroughs, supernatural phenomena, total victory in every battle and end of suffering.

One key element in Divine remembrance is the principle of Divine timing. God moves according to His timing, which is absolutely accurate; He is never too late and never too early. Lazarus was dead and buried for four days, but Jesus visited his grave and resurrected Lazarus (John chapter 11). It may seem that you have been forgotten, written off, abandoned, or that your blessings are delayed, but God has not forgotten you, nor His promises concerning you. At the appropriate time, He will remember and visit you. Be sure that: your expectation will not be cut off (Prov. 24:14).

↳ my God will do everything He said He would concerning me

The time for God to remember you has come. This is the time God has purposed to remember, visit and favour you and to actualise your destiny. Thou shalt arise and have mercy upon Zion; for the time to favour her, yea, the set time is come (Psalm 102: 13). We are told that God remembered and visited Noah, Abraham, Sarah, Joseph, Hannah, Job, Daniel, Mordecai and Elizabeth. He will remember you too! You have a responsibility however. You can provoke God to remember you speedily. Thus, your expectation can become manifestation. Hannah's prayer in Shiloh provoked God to remember her "And Elkanah knew Hannah his wife; and the Lord remembered her" (1 Sam. 1:19). Your positive and persistent prayer, trust in God, patience and purity of life can provoke God to remember you and re-write the story of your life.

↓ remember that its even his grace that even gets you to pray

Pastor B.B. Olagunju's book, "Remember Me" is unique, practical, timely, thoroughly biblical and prophetic. He has written from his wealth of pastoral experience from three perspectives. Firstly, he explains the essence of "Divine Remembrance" from biblical perspectives. Secondly, he encourages all Christians, using biblical and contemporary examples to feel a sense of belonging and being Divinely remembered. Finally, he challenges us to provoke God to remember us. He has provided some feasible, practical and biblical tips that can supernaturally transform your life, if faithfully applied.

The book is loaded with scriptural truths and revelations; it is easy to read and understand, yet it is profound in its contents and presentation. I urge you, not only to read this book, but to patiently digest it, diligently apply it to your life and faithfully pass it on. You will never be the same again!

Rev. Dr. G. A. Christopher.

General overseer:
WorldWide Missionary Gospel Church,
Lagos State, Nigeria, West Africa.

This book is a priceless tool that gives practical encouragement in every sphere of life. A unique revelation and exposition of the word of knowledge is offered to you in Pastor BB Olagunju's timeless book, "Remember Me." Whatever challenges you may be facing, you are assured of being refreshed and renewed in your spirit to face each day with confidence and hope. It is refreshing to know that God is still on the throne and He remembers you every second! Yes, He remembers you! He can never forget you because He has you in the palm of His hand. Therefore, keep a good attitude of faith and be positive that He'll breathe new hope and strength into your spirit as you read this book. Colossians 3:2 counsels, "Set your minds and keep them set on what is above." I encourage you to grab copies for yourself and your loved ones. No matter what is going on around you, choose to believe that God is near and He remembers you in the chapters of His books. Enjoy this masterpiece!

Pastor (Mrs) Benedicta Olagunju

Dedication

I would like to dedicate this book to my God, the Giver or Life, who's Grace has sustained me to date. I would also like to dedicate this book to my parents Prince Joseph Ajibade Olagunju and Princess Johanna Ayoola Olagunju. They have both gone to be with the Lord, but their parenthood brought me to the true knowledge of God who I will serve forever.

I am also delighted to dedicate this book to the love of my life, my wife Benedicta Gbemisola Olagunju, the most profound and godly woman I have ever known. Her total commitment to Jesus, her courageous spirit and her incredible love for me and the people God committed to me, has inspired me and strengthened me. She is fearless; yet tender, full of joy and passion.

Without her I do not believe I could have carried the cross of my Call this far. It is an awesome joy living my life with you my love.

Finally, I dedicate this book to my children and my grand daughter; Maria, Benedict, Michael, Deborah and Johanna. I am blessed to have you all in my life. You have never complained, you love what I love, and hate what I hate; children, I love you all with passion.

And to all who feel forgotten...

Foreword

It is easy to feel forgotten in life and when we feel forgotten we lose our enthusiasm. Have you ever felt forgotten and left behind? Well, one thing that I can guarantee as a certainty is that you are not forgotten! God has not forgotten about you so get your hopes fired up today; you are unforgettable to God and He will never leave you nor forsake you.

The phrase "God remembers you" is found 73 times in the Scripture. The main idea which this book intends to imprint on our minds is the message that when God remembers a person, He usually does something positive, redemptive and life changing for such a person – see Psalms 105:42. People may leave you when you need them the most, but God is the friend that sticks closer than a brother. His intervention always brings a definite change, deliverance and new beginnings in a person's life. The benefits of His remembrance are very far reaching, bringing uncommon blessings, causing the accuser of the brethren to be dispersed and provoking restoration of destinies.

As far as God is concerned, when He remembers a person, their past -whatever it had been - becomes immaterial, people around them including the community in which they dwell share in the benefits of Gods provision. When God remembers, He blesses with His favour; God is so merciful that He remembers the dreams He has put in your heart and why He made you. He remembers your purpose in life, God knows your purpose and He is not going to write you off so expect your dreams in life to happen, believe in God as your Creator because Jehovah Remembers! And when God remembers you, all the forces of darkness cannot keep you from fulfilling your purpose.

As in everything that God does in our lives, we are reminded of some cooperative actions required on our part which may be necessary for God's remembrance in our lives. While it is God's sovereign act to remember us, we have a responsibility to provoke such a remembrance. We need a cooperating relationship with God to get Him to do what He delights in doing in our lives

Bear in mind that as God remembers us, we must remember all His goodness in our lives - both past and present and maintain a thankful heart. As believers we ought to be thankful for everything including the things we often take for granted. There may be things He is yet to do for us in His infinite wisdom however; we need to be grateful for that which He has done. By being grateful for what He has done and being thankful in the throes of the challenges that we face in life, we provoke Him to remember us.

In a succinct but simple way, this book is an encouragement and a reminder for us to get involved with God in His work in our lives and on our behalf.

Introduction

The word 'remember' has been defined as two things – to call to mind after a period of absence from the mind, or to keep in mind continuously.

To remember is:

> lto be capable of recalling when required; to keep in mind; to be continually aware or thoughtful of; to preserve fresh in the memory; to attend to; to think of with gratitude, affection, respect, or any other emotion. E.g. "Remember the Sabbath day, to keep it holy." *Ex.20 v 8"* (Selfknowledege.com)

It also means to:

recall to the mind with effort; think of again: e.g. '*I finally remembered the address*'; to recall or become aware of suddenly or spontaneously: e.g. '*Then I remembered that today is your birthday*'; to retain in the memory: e.g. *Remember your appointment*; to keep (someone) in mind as worthy of consideration or recognition. (freedictionary.com)

Remembrance has been regularly and more commonly used to signify recalling something or someone to mind after a period of absence. As the above definitions have shown, the word remember or remembrance also signifies a continual awareness of someone or something; keeping that person or thing fresh in one's memory.

Remembrance or 'to remember' could therefore be an active process act i.e. one where there is an event of recollection or a passive act i.e. one where there is a continuing presence in the mind.

In addition to these definitions of remembrance, divine remembrance is indicative of a time when God brings people out of a situation that they have been in for some amount of time, no matter how short or longer lasting the situation has persisted for.

'Remembrance' is a time of 'coming out' and it is symbolic of a certain or definite time in the life of a person when God deals with their situation. This was Noah's experience when God remembered him and all who were with him in the ark and He brought them out of the Ark **(Gen 8v1).** This was the time in the life of Noah when God brought him out of his confinement in the ark!

> *"But God remembered Noah and all the wild animals and the livestock that were with him in the ark, and he sent a wind over the earth, and the waters receded.....By the twenty-seventh day of the second month the earth was completely dry. Then God said to Noah, "Come out of the ark, you and your wife and your sons and their wives".*
> **(Gen 8v14-16)**

The season of remembrance in the dictionary of God represents a time to be remembered or a time 'to come out'. If you have felt forgotten, left behind or ignored or indeed you feel God is no longer on your side, I want to assure you that God still knows your name, He knows where you live and He has not forgotten your name. Your season of remembrance is on hand! The contents of this book will reassure you that God has not, can not and has never forgotten you as we see in our first definition of the word 'remember'!

Chapter 1

Divine remembrance is the time and season in a person's life when God brings them out of their trying situation; it is the bringing in or beginning of a blessing to any man or woman. If any person is remembered by God in this life, it means that the time for them to be blessed has come! No one has ever tasted the blessings of God in any area of their lives whether matrimonially, financially, in their careers or spiritually without having been remembered by God. When God remembers a man, it simply means that he has been visited by God. A time of remembrance is that season in a persons life when it can be said that they have arrived in the spirit. A man can not be said to have been remembered until God blesses him, and I am not referring simply to being blessed financially or materially but in all other areas as well. As Prov 10:22 puts it, "The blessing of the LORD makes one rich, And He adds no sorrow with it".

God remembered a certain woman in the Bible who was a non-entity – a 'nobody' until that point of remembrance. It is recorded in the book of Genesis chapter 30 verse 22 that:

> *"And God remembered Rachel; He listened to her and opened her womb".*

Rachel was recorded as a woman who picked quarrels and physical fights with her husband because she was childless. Before she was remembered of God, Rachel was a bitter fruitless and childless woman, a woman who should not be reckoned with. When God remembered her however, she became the mother of two great nations that we always make mention of when we preach the gospel of our Lord Jesus Christ. Rachel became the proud mother of Joseph - the prime minister of Egypt, the biggest and greatest empire of that time (see Gen 41:41). She was also the mother of Benjamin; who was head and progenitor of the tribe that produced the first king of Israel as recorded in the Bible (see 1Sam 9:1). Bible studies also reveal that Paul who wrote half of the New Testament, descended from the lineage of that man Benjamin born to Rachel when she was remembered by God (see Rom 11:1b).

when God remembers somebody, their situation will change dramatically for the better! I am convinced that there is change on the horizon for you. Recently, a member of my church called me on the phone and asked me to pray for her as she was about to go for her practical driving test for the eighth time, I said not a problem, you go ahead and go for your test, I will pray as you have asked. I joined hands with my wife and we prayed for her concerning her driving test, she called me again later that week to confirm with tears of joy that she had finally passed her driving test at the eight time of asking, God remembered her! Child of God, I declare to you that when your time comes and God remembers you, there is nothing anyone can do about it. You will come out of that situation you have been in.

Does God Actually Forget?

There are five references in the Bible where it is recorded that "God remembered": **Gen 8:1** God remembered Noah, **Gen 19:29** He remembered Abraham, **Gen 30:22**, God remembered Rachel, **Ex 2:24** He remembered His covenant with Abraham and Isaac and with Jacob and **1sam 1:19** Elkanah knew his wife and the Lord remembered her. You might possibly be asking and wondering what I mean when I say God 'remembered' because the word itself tends to suggest that God forgot or lost sight of an issue or a person and had to be reminded about them but this is not the case.

When I say that God remembered Noah, and other people in the Bible, it does not mean that God forgot about these people, that He neglected these people - NO and absolutely No! On the contrary, these people and their plight were ever before God. As we see in the definition of the word remember earlier on, God kept these people in mind; He was continually aware and thoughtful of them; and He preserved them fresh in His memory! It is impossible for God to forget anyone of His children or anyone of His people. He is too organised to forget about you. He is mighty, infinite and described as the omniscient God who knows all things to the finest details. When the Bible says He knows all things, He knows everything to the very smallest detail. He is interested in every strand of hair on your head (see **Matt 10:30)**, when you go to the barbers every week to shave off your hair; God knows the very numbering of the hair that falls off your head, He knows that it is hair number 11,106!

It reminds me of a man of God who at the young age of 30 began to lose his hair rapidly for some strange reason, his wife had began to tease him that he would be using a wig very shortly, one day as he stood in the toilet combing his hair, strands of hair were falling off as he combed so he picked them up, put them on top of his head and commanded the hair to grow back in the name of Jesus and to back this up, he quoted the scripture in Luke chapter 12 verse 7 and Matthew chapter 10 verse 30 that said He knows the number of hair on our head and according to that word from the Bible, he commanded a growth of the hair on his head and within weeks, every trace of baldness on his head was reversed! This goes to show you that God knows and cares about the smallest of issues that we face every day. He can never ever forget about you, in the book of Isaiah chapter 49, people were saying the same thing, that God had forgotten them but God had a response for every one of them, let's look at what He said:

> But Zion said, "The LORD has forsaken me, the Lord has forgotten me." "Can a mother forget the baby at her breast and have no compassion on the child she has borne? Though she may forget, I will not forget you! See, I have engraved you on the palms of my hands; your walls are ever before me
> (*Is 49:14-16 NIV*)

Is it possible for a mother to forget a suckling child? Back in the day, I would have said emphatically that this was impossible but in this present generation, one readily sees parents who abandon their children and treat them with extreme cruelty but God says, even if a mother can possibly forget a child that she has borne yet will I never forget you! The Bible says that we are inscribed in the palm of His hands, there is absolutely no way He can ever forget you or me.

Some women have inadvertently suffocated their children as they slept because either in their sleep or in their tiredness, they forgot that the baby was lying beside them but God will never forget you whether deliberately or unwittingly because He says "I have inscribed you in the palm of my hands and your walls are ever before me!" He knows the balance in your bank account, the outstanding amount on your mortgage, every scar on your body and every single thing you have had to deal with in this life. In the book of Isaiah chapter 44 verse 21, God declares:

> "Pay attention, O Jacob and Israel, for you are my servant, O Israel. I, the LORD, made you, and I will not forget you". (NLT)

You are God's Israel (if you are born again) and He knows your name and exactly what your needs are and He will not leave you helpless but will show up for you.

🌿

Chapter 2

ACTIVATING GOD'S REMEMBRANCE

Now that we have established that God cannot forget His children, let me share the outcome of my research into the Bible about people who were remembered.

The term *"and God remembered"* appears five times in the Bible, I researched around each of these instances where that statement was made in the Bible. Here is a list of these instances before we proceed:

In Gen 8:1 *"and God remembered Noah and all the living things in the ark"*

Gen 19:29 *"and God remembered Abraham"*

Gen 30:22*"and God remembered Rachel's plea"*

Exodus 2:24 *"and God remembered his covenant with Abraham Isaac and Jacob"*

1 Sam 1:19*"Elkanah slept with his wife and God remembered her and she bore a son".*

So there you have the instances when the phrase "and God remembered" is used, and having studied all these instances, I noted three things in particular that all these people referred to in the scriptures have in common: three things that they all did before God was recorded as remembering them. Please bear in mind as you read this text that we have established that God did not in literal terms forget about these people in the first instance but there came a time when God acted on their cases and brought them out of their circumstances. It is clear to me that we as individuals have a role to play if God will remember us in a similar manner and if we will do these three things that these people mentioned in the scriptures did, we would get Heaven's attention.

EFFECTUAL FERVENT PRAYER

> [1] *The effectual fervent prayer of a righteous man availeth much".*
>
> James 5:16b

One of the first things I noted about these people which we need to learn from is that they prayed fervently and even violently! The place of prayer can not be neglected if you want to turn God's attention towards you and your situation. Don't limit your prayers or your praying to the house of God. All the time Noah was in the ark, he was praying and it came to the second month of the year when God remembered him. Noah is noted to have been a friend of God and I am convinced that he must have been praying throughout his stay in the ark, I don't believe he simply sat back waiting for things to take their natural course. The adage that "When all is said and done, more is still expected to be done" rang true with Noah so he must have been praying that the food supplies would not run out and that things will work out smoothly considering that he was sharing the ark with lions and other predatory animals who could easily turn on him and his family if not properly fed.

Pray with an expectation

Consider Hannah, Elkanah's wife who went to Shiloh yearly with her family (i.e. her husband and her husband's wife and children). Imagine the pain and shame she had to endure at the hands of Peninah and at the hands of Peninah's children. Imagine the ridicule she had to deal with as the family approached Shiloh every year, just imagine what Peninah and her children must have been saying to her yearly. Every year she went to Shiloh with an expectation and in prayer. It is useless to come to church and to come to the place of prayer without having an expectation that what you are praying for will become a reality, it can almost be described as foolishness and stupidity. Don't ever come into God's house or His presence without an expectation:

> "And without faith it is impossible to please God, because anyone who comes to him must believe that he exists and that he rewards those who earnestly seek him".
> Heb 11:6
>
> "If you believe, you will receive whatever you ask for in prayer". Matt 21:22

(Also see Psalm 55:16, Psalm 56:9, 1 John 5:14 and Prov 23:18).

Hannah had been visiting Shiloh yearly without an expectation; she went to Shiloh as a religious duty. Indeed there was no record that in all her visits to Shiloh and to God's house that she ever prayed, it would appear that she simply went year after year to offer the prescribed sacrifice to fulfil all righteousness and afterwards she went home to quarrel with her husband and to be bitter about her barrenness and Peninah's fruitfulness.

When you go before the presence of the Almighty, be sure to go before Him with an expectation; with a desire to receive something from Him. Until Hannah came to the realisation that she needed to communicate with Him and to strike a deal with the Almighty, she continued to go into His presence yearly simply as a routine. In spite of the fact that Sunday is generally regarded as a day for regular religious gathering of Christians, when you come to such gatherings or services, determine in your heart that you will receive something from him, determine in your heart and have an expectation that you will be blessed with your heart's desire.

The lack of expectation seems to have been the reason for the delay in Hannah's life – the delay in receiving a child into her arms. She came to the realisation eventually that she needed to speak to the Most High and to trust Him to fulfil her heart's desire and meet her expectation.

Pray in the Spirit

When she got to that place that particular year, she prayed such a heartfelt and deeply moving prayer that her lips could not mouth the words; her voice could not carry the anguish in her soul. She tapped into something that was meant for and reserved for New Testament Christians as recorded in **Romans chapter 8 verse 26,** she prayed in the Spirit!

> *"In the same way, the Spirit helps us in our weakness. We do not know what we ought to pray for, but the Spirit himself intercedes for us with groans that words cannot express".* Rom 8:26

Praying in the Spirit is a benefit that we as New Testament Christians are blessed with. This is a gift and an ability to speak in new tongues including speaking in the tongues or language of angels in order to communicate unhindered, uninterrupted and un-opposed with the Father. It is a heavenly ability to pray prayers that even our minds are not big enough to comprehend or understand.

The Bible states that after Hannah's episode of prayer in the temple that "God remembered her". Child of God, I believe every one of us have things that we are dealing with in our individual lives. There are things that people are lacking in their lives because they have failed to deal with the 'lack' by spending appropriate time praying to the Almighty Father for whom nothing is too difficult - who is able to do all things and would only give good gifts to His children.

> "*Is anything too hard for the LORD?*"
> Gen 18:14a
>
> "*Every good and perfect gift is from above, coming down from the Father of the heavenly lights, who does not change like shifting shadows*". James 1:17

A lot of Christians are yet to take advantage of the gift of speaking in tongues that will enable them to tackle and pray for those things that are standing in their way, things they can not know about by operating only in the physical realm. The Bible says that our fight is not against flesh and blood....

> "For we wrestle not against flesh and blood, but against principalities, against powers, against the rulers of the darkness of this world, against spiritual wickedness in high places". Eph 6:12

And the weapons that we are to fight with are not the natural ones, not a simple prayer in English or your local dialect but fight and pray with spiritual weapons....

> "For the weapons of our warfare are not physical [weapons of flesh and blood], but they are mighty before God for the overthrow and destruction of strongholds".
> **(2 Cor. 10:4)**

Hannah prayed from her heart and I always stress and encourage people to pray in the Holy Spirit. When you pray in the Spirit, even if your eyes are open during prayer, you do not see things around you because you are praying in the Spirit. Hannah's violent prayers led to her to remembrance, it caused God to remember her!

> *"In bitterness of soul Hannah wept much and prayed to the LORD. And she made a vow, saying, "O LORD Almighty, if you will only look upon your servant's misery and remember me, and not forget your servant but give her a son, then I will give him to the LORD for all the days of his life, and no razor will ever be used on his head." As she kept on praying to the LORD, Eli observed her mouth. Hannah was praying in her heart, and her lips were moving but her voice was not heard….Elkanah lay with Hannah his wife, and the LORD remembered her.* 1 Sam 1 10-13, 19b

There are certain problems you are facing that can not be dealt with other than by effectual and fervent praying in the Holy Ghost, some things require prayer and fasting! Even the Lord Jesus stated that some things only go out by prayer and by fasting (see Matt 17:21). You must attack those things that seem to have defied every other solution by violent prayers with fasting; you must pray with all your might when you are addressing things that refuse to go away and make it seem as if God has abandoned you, things that seem unmoveable. Psalm 56 verse 9 declares that the day I cried out, my enemy will turn back and know the Lord is for me! When you cry out in prayer, something will happen for you and a change will come.

Like a woman in childbirth

Child of God, are there things that have remained the same in your life because you have refused to cry out to God? Is there an enemy pursuing after you that is gaining the advantage over you because you have refused to cry out? Well, consider the scripture in Isaiah 42:14

> "For a long time I have kept silent, I have been quiet and held myself back. **But now, like a woman in childbirth, I cry out,** I gasp and pant"
> (emphasis mine)

Women in childbirth don't care about anything, they don't care about looking pretty and they don't care who is looking or not, they cry out without shame! I recall one of my experiences with my wife in a labour ward, she screamed out in pain and I said to her, darling just continue speaking in tongues, she looked at me and said tongues? She screamed out again in vernacular YEeeeeeeeeeeeeeeeeeee! with no decorum whatsoever. Just like a woman in childbirth, you must be able to scream out and seek the face of the Lord with intensity and not care for what is happening around you. I pray that the Lord will give you the ability to cry unto Him violently, that He will give you the ability to come into His presence with great expectation! Cry unto to Him and you will see the power of remembrance in your life.

Chapter 3

EXERCISE PATIENCE

The second thing I noticed in the lives of those recorded as being remembered in the Bible is that they were patient in waiting for the Lord. Lots of people are not in the habit of waiting for the Lord; a lot of us can pray, pray fervently, pray in the Spirit but can not wait. A good number of Christians do not fall foul of failing to pray fervently, neither do they fall foul of having a desire or an expectation to receive from God, rather a lot of Christians do not know or understand what it means to be patient. This is evident in our marriages and homes where people or couples can no longer wait when faced with trying times, we are not patient to work and wait in order to make things better in our marriages. People do not realise that marriage could mean 'mileage', a distance to go that will require endurance.

A recent survey showed that only 3 out of 15 marriages are still in existence at the time a child born in the first year of the relationship becomes five years old. That is, 4 in 5 (80%) of marriages would have packed up within its first five years. I worked out the numbers and I said this is terrible! Simply because we can not wait, we fail to recognise that a husband and a wife are from two different backgrounds and need to work out their relationship to achieve harmony and a blend.

When you knock or hammer a nail into wood in order to join or 'couple' two pieces of wood together, it does not simply slide in smoothly; the resistance from the wood itself ensures that the nail holds the wood firmly. If there is no resistance or friction when you hammer the nail in, it is suggestive of the fact that the nail will not hold firm enough in the wood to ensure a firm joint. On the other hand, it also suggests that more effort is required to get the nail in firmly, so all parties must be willing to put in the extra effort to work through the difficulties and all kinds of resistance to build a firm and solid relationship. Couples must work it out before they can 'couple' and blend. (see Prov 27:17)

Competing with the Jones'

Another proof that we are not good at waiting in this generation is the desire of people to be like the 'Jones". People see their peers and persons that they grew up with or started out with, doing very well financially, materially or otherwise and immediately, they feel the need and compulsion to compete or match the achievement of their peers. This is generally done blindly as those who compare themselves with others have no clue, no idea how the person they are comparing themselves with achieved their so-called great wealth! The Bible says people who do this are foolish people!

> *But they measuring themselves by themselves, and comparing themselves among themselves, are not wise".* 2 Cor. 10:12 KJV

In trying to measure up to the Jones', people have dabbled into illegal and criminal activities in order to amass wealth and measure up to their peers! There was a man on an African TV channel recently who went to a traditional spiritualist; he wanted to find out if and when he would be rich. The spiritualist told him he would actually be rich but he needed to wait for another year to see this happen. This man said one year was too long a time for him to wait, he insisted that the spiritualist must be able to do something to make him rich right away, eventually the spiritualist gave in and said there might be a way to do this, he went into his inner room only to return with a miniature coffin. He gave this to the man and said the coffin must be supplied with human blood every year, the first person to die as a result of this ritual was his father, and then his brother and so death passed through the family in order for this man to become wealthy immediately and remain wealthy. Nothing that the devil gives to you is free; there is always a hidden price and because this man could not wait and refused to be patient for things to take a natural course (see Job 14:14), he brought an early death to his family.

Patience gets Heaven's Attention

In the Bible, there are classical examples of three people who waited on God and their patience resulted in God Himself making a definite and remarkable statement about them. Since I discovered this truth in the Bible I have been greatly encouraged, inspired and cheered up. I no longer worry about delay in my life, it doesn't move me when things don't happen when I want them to and I can not be intimidated to do things because others are doing them.

Firstly, there was Jesus Christ, who could have achieved His work on earth at age 18, 21 or any other age but instead waited for the opportune time; He waited for 33 good years before He accomplished

His purpose. Thirty three and a half years it took Him before He went to the cross; He endured everything on the earth for the opportune time. As a result of His patience, after His baptism by John the Baptist, the Bible records that a voice came from heaven declaring:

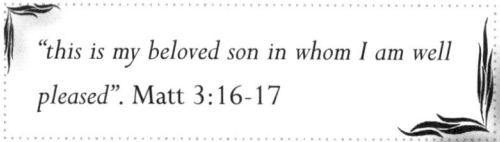

> *"this is my beloved son in whom I am well pleased".* Matt 3:16-17

Even when He was on the cross, Jesus endured the insults and the agony He was put through before His death until the right time as arranged by God.

Secondly, apart from Jesus, I also studied the man called Abraham. God made him a promise at age 75;

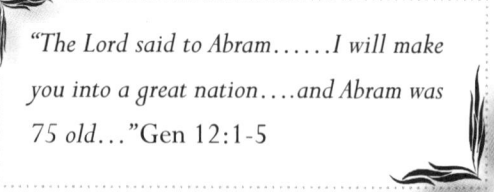

> *"The Lord said to Abram......I will make you into a great nation....and Abram was 75 old..."* Gen 12:1-5

The promise did not come to pass until he was a hundred years old;

> *"Abraham was a hundred years old when his son Isaac was born to him".* Gen 21:5

He waited for an entire twenty five year period before he received the son he was promised.

And thirdly, there was the man called David in the Bible who was anointed king over Israel at the tender age of 16 as the last born son of Jesse, in his father's front room when the prophet Samuel visited and poured the oil from the special horn on him. He waited for a total of fourteen years before he actually ascended to the throne, this was despite having numerous opportunities to seize power from King Saul or indeed to take the life of King Saul and ascend to the throne. David chose instead to be patient and to wait on God and this is what God said about him;

> *"I have found a man after my own heart"*
> Acts 13:22

When you can wait patiently on the Lord, there will be direct comments from Heaven about you; there will be a direct mention of you by God Himself. God will remember you and all that you are going through when you choose to wait on Him.

In our day and in our generation, we have all adopted a microwave mindset where we can't seem to wait for anything. Those three people waited and were remembered. When you are waiting on the Lord, people may start to make snide remarks about you such as: 'look at you, over forty years old and no wife to show for it, all your hair has already gone grey but no wife or children to show for it' but I tell you just wait on God because in the fullness of time, you will not only get married but in addition to getting married God will bless you and you will produce twins! True patience is waiting without worrying. God cannot forget you, all you need to do is learn to wait on Him and when you are waiting like Noah of old, God will remember. I say it again; God will definitely remember you as you wait patiently on Him.

> "I waited patiently for the LORD;
> he turned to me and heard my cry".
> Psalm 40:1

Chapter 4

LIVE IN THE LIGHT OF THE WORD

The third thing I want to talk about in addition to praying violently, and waiting patiently on God, is that there is a need for us to live in the Light of God and in the Light of His Word. Whilst praying and whilst waiting on God, we need to live pure, transparent and holy lives:

> "Make every effort to live in peace with all men and to be holy; without holiness no one will see the Lord". Heb12:14

A lot of Christians live dodgy lifestyles and then they go ahead and misrepresent things even to their pastors. A member of my congregation admitted this to me sometime ago and stated that it was common practice amongst Christians. I know this to be true for a fact but there is no substitute to living a holy life as a Christian.

A lot of us don't live a good life, our lives are not transparent, and our lives can be described as opaque and dodgy! Very frosty and clouded or beclouded! May God help us as His children to walk and live in the Light and in the truth of His Word in Jesus Name. We must learn to live transparent and holy lives because we are children of the Light.

> *"You are all sons of the light and sons of the day. We do not belong to the night or to the darkness".* 1 Thessalonians 5:5

When I saw that scripture, I made a link between it and John 8:12. Jesus said:

> *"Whilst I am in the world, I am the light of the world",*
>
> *"Whilst it is day, I will do the work of my father".* John 9:5
>
> *"To as many as believed on him, He gave them the power to become the sons of God".* John 1:12

Gossip can becloud your life

The day you believed on Him, you became His child and therefore a child of the Light who is meant to do the work of the Father just like Jesus! We are meant to do the work of the Light, we are meant to live transparent lives. When waiting on God, we must be true to the Light, if you are waiting for a husband, you should not be dating two men at the same time; that is dodgy! That is immoral. Our lives need to be transparent; if you want God to remember you, you must of necessity learn to live a transparent life! Tell things exactly the way they are; don't embellish the story; don't make up different versions of it for different audiences. Don't speak evil of people behind their backs and smile at them when they walk onto the scene! Most people do not approve of gossip, but enjoying it is enough to defile you.

God woke me up in the middle of the night once and said to me, 'do you know you may hate that person, but I love them'. I said to God, "what do you mean sir?" He said to me, "when you walk and work amongst Christians, i.e. when you operate within a church community, the devil will tempt you to hate and dislike Christians because they are human beings as well as being Christians. They are not perfect so they will make mistakes and do things that will offend you and you will constantly have opportunity to hate or despise them; to talk bad about them and be loathsome of them. However you are simply wasting your time because, even though you hate and despise any of them, I love them dearly! Since that experience, I have been consciously careful of what I say about God's people and how I treat God's people. I determined that no matter what is going on with any Christian, and no matter what they say or do, I will pray for them, love them and that will be the end of that.

Many Christians have no friends or enemies except in the house of God because that is the community within which they operate. You may dislike me or hate me for example for one reason or the other but recognise that God loves me, just as much as He loves any other member of the Christendom who you hold something against. You are wasting your time hating me for example because God loves me dearly. Anything I say or do in church ends in church. I don't carry things around and moan and gripe about them because as God has shown me by revelation, such actions are a complete waste of time! I will never sit down with anyone to gossip or talk about another, that should never be something that Christians do! We must strive to live transparent lives!

As Christians, operating amongst Christians, don't make it a habit to talk about other Christians or about your pastor, slandering them! Slandering the very one who prays for you and blesses you, slandering the sister or brother who takes out time to pray for you in the prayer group! (See 1Thess 5:12-13) This is a waste of time! Though you may dislike or hate that person, God loves them dearly and all your hate and slander is a waste of your time! People who do such things are not living or demonstrating transparent lives! I say it again; we must live lives that are pure, holy and transparent if we want God to remember us! (See Habakkuk 1:13)

Living in the Light takes you to the top

Look at the life of Joseph, one of the people God remembered in the Bible as recorded in the book of Genesis Chapter 39 Verse 9. Whatever thing you are doing in your closet is the very thing that will transpire in your outward life. Joseph is an example of a man who lived a transparent life. When he was in a dark room having been lured by Potiphar's wife, he said to himself, 'how can I do such a thing and sin against God?' Though his secret would have been safe in that dark place if he had succumbed to his master's wife, he opted to be holy instead.

A lot of us are married yet we have masquerades outside in the name of mistresses and concubines, this is not a transparent lifestyle, no adulterer will inherit the kingdom of God (Rev 21:8) and God does not remember people who live such lives. You can be waiting on God for years for an answer but when your life is not pure or transparent; you will fail to draw God's attention to your plight. You can continue to come to church and still nothing will happen. It is my prayer that God will remove from everyone reading this text anything that makes their life impure in the Name of Jesus. I pray that any evil way in you that is causing you to live a forgotten life, in a place where it seems God has forgotten you, will be taken away from you by God in the name of Jesus.

Even when Joseph was thrown into the prison following his encounter with Potiphar's wife, it was made known publicly that he lived a transparent life when he was made the head of the prisoners because people who are of questionable character are not given noble positions much less a position where they are charged with the responsibility of looking after other prisoners whose desire is to seek freedom!

> *"So the warden put Joseph in charge of all those held in the prison, and he was made responsible for all that was done there".*
> Gen 39:22

If Joseph was a person of questionable character, he could not have been trusted to stand guard over the other prisoners when he could have himself orchestrated a jail break! As a result of his transparent life, God set things up for Joseph beginning with the cup bearer's dream (see Gen 40:5), then came Pharaoh's troubling dream a couple of years later (see Gen 41:1). I encourage you to realise that nothing that you do for God, none of your labour for Him will go in vain, God will certainly reward you for everything you do in honour of Him.

Be prepared to help others achieve their dreams

Joseph helped the cupbearer by interpreting his dream; bear in mind that the cupbearer did not go to Joseph but the Bible records that Joseph noticed that the countenance of the cupbearer was downcast – Joseph had a genuine interest and cared for the welfare of those around him (Prov 27:23). This is an attribute that I encourage Christians to have; it is an attribute that I demonstrate in my service as a Pastor. If I know you to be lively and bubbly and notice that your heart is heavy especially if I notice it on more than one occasion, I will seek to find out if anything is wrong and perhaps God will use me to say a word of encouragement to lift such a person's spirit. A lot of people appreciate it but others actually either take advantage of this or despise me for being caring (or over shepherding as they call it) nevertheless, God's work must be done!

It was Joseph who recognised that the cupbearer was not his usual self, he prodded and encouraged the cupbearer to share his burden and as soon as the cupbearer mentioned that he was troubled as a result of a dream, Joseph said, tell me your dream and God will give you an interpretation of it through me! We know the rest of the story how he gave an accurate interpretation of the dream and the cupbearer was restored to his position. Joseph had asked the cupbearer to remember him when he was restored but Joseph in his youthful exuberance did not realise that it is only God he could rely on to remember him or indeed cause him to be remembered.

Only God can cause you to be remembered

The cupbearer completely forgot Joseph until God Himself caused Pharaoh to have a troubling dream. Even when this happened, the cupbearer still did not remember Joseph! Wise man after wise man and soothsayer after soothsayer came into Pharaoh's presence and each time they could not interpret the dream, the cupbearer stood there helpless with no recollection of the man called Joseph who had interpreted his dream. It is clear that God wanted to share His glory with no man because it was only after every wise man in the land had an opportunity to interpret the dream and they had all failed, that the cupbearer finally came to his senses and said to his troubled master,

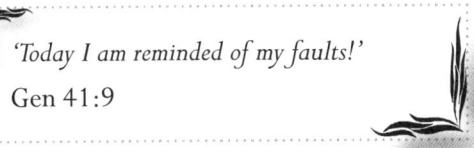

> *'Today I am reminded of my faults!'*
> Gen 41:9

Who do you think made this cupbearer to remember Joseph? *It was God!*

The cupbearer further said to Pharaoh 'there is a man I met in prison who interpreted my dreams and his interpretation of my dream was accurate!' Pharaoh was so desperate at this point that he didn't care where the interpretation came from; he immediately ordered that Joseph be released and brought to him. If the cupbearer had remembered Joseph before Pharaoh had consulted all the wise men in the land, Pharaoh would have probably shown no interest in speaking to a jailbird about his very troubling dream when there were wise men in the land to be consulted.

→ but be genuine

When you make things happen for others, when you live such a transparent and holy life that can not be faulted, God will set things up for your upliftment. When Joseph was summoned, he did not appear before the king in his prison clothes, no! He took the time to clean up and he was dressed up to stand before the

King! I pray that as you live a transparent life before God even in your closet or secret place, God will cause you to be clothed with good things to stand before great men in Jesus Name. God will set you up for a royal audience in Jesus Name! AMEN!

When God remembers a man, no one and nothing can stop him, what people say or think will be of no concern to God. I declare that your set time to be blessed is here.

> 'and God remembered Noah and all the living things'. Gen 8:1

Noah had been in the ark for quite a while, he had not heard from God since he shut the doors of the ark having obeyed God's instructions to go into the ark with all manner of animals; but when the time came, God remembered him and all that were with him and He said to him, you are remembered, come out. I declare concerning you as a son and servant of the Most High God, I prophesy that as God remembered Noah and commanded him to come out of the predicament he was in, God will remember you in your predicament and He will speak to you and your situation and will bring you out in Jesus Name. As God spoke to Noah and said 'step out', I declare that you will step out of your situation into glory in Jesus Name! After Noah came out, all that was evil around him had been destroyed and humanity had a fresh start (see Isaiah 42:9b), I decree that every evil thing standing against you will be destroyed by the power of the Almighty and you will have a glorious fresh start in Jesus Name. Walk free into a life filled with testimonies in the Name of Jesus!

Chapter 5

BENEFITS OF BEING REMEMBERED BY GOD

We have considered some of the things that we can do to bring God's remembrance into our lives. We have looked at the lives of the likes of our fore father Abraham, David and our Lord Jesus Christ. Let us now look at a few benefits of being remembered.

Let us look at the book of Exodus chapter 33 verse 19

"And the LORD said, "I will cause all my goodness to pass in front of you, and I will proclaim my name, the LORD, in your presence. I will have mercy on whom I will have mercy, and I will have compassion on whom I will have compassion".

Before we go into the detail of this section, let me first advise you to replace the word 'you' in that verse with your name i.e. 'I will cause my goodness to pass before Pastor BB Olagunju and I will proclaim my name (Jehovah Elshaddai) in the presence of Pastor Olagunju and I will have mercy on him!'

There comes a time when God remembers His people by name, a time when God places the file of his people before Himself and declares it is time to act and remedy that situation! In the preceding chapters, we have been looking at divine remembrance, and what happens when God remembers His people. We will now further that discussion in the same direction of the things we should expect to happen or the benefits we should expect to accrue to us on account of being remembered by God.

It is recorded in the book of Esther chapter 6 verses 1 & 2 as follows:

> *"That night the king could not sleep; so he ordered the book of the chronicles, the record of his reign, to be brought in and read to him. It was found recorded there that Mordecai had exposed Bigthana and Teresh, two of the king's officers who guarded the doorway, who had conspired to assassinate King Xerxes"*

It is my earnest desire and prayer that as Mordecai was remembered by the King that God will cause someone in the corridors of power to have sleepless nights in order to bring about a performance of every favour that is due unto you in Jesus Name.

REMEMBRANCE BRINGS A BLESSING

We learnt in the previous chapters that when God blesses a man, he is divinely remembered, conversely when God divinely remembers a man, He blesses him. We have all been blessed in some form or another; we have all been blessed to varying degrees, this is an indication of God's remembrance in our lives. It is a grace we have to be here and alive today, To be married, to have children or to have a job is by the grace of God. It has nothing to do with your own ability – the horse may be ready for the day of battle but victory comes from the Lord. God's grace manifested in our lives is proof of God's remembrance in our lives.

Divine remembrance or blessing starts with God remembering a person and for the purpose of this chapter, I will use another woman who for so many years was trusting God for the fruit of the womb, her name was Rachel, married to Jacob – the son of Isaac, the son of Abraham. She had made physical, emotional and even spiritual attempts to get pregnant with her husband's help but none of this had worked for her. Her sister Leah (also married to Jacob) was producing babies like a machine on a yearly basis and giving them names that served to taunt poor old Rachel. The Bible records that on one occasion, Rachel got physical with her husband and said 'give me a child or I die' but nothing happened, until God remembered her! She didn't realise that having a child is not by power or might but by the spirit of the Lord (Zechariah 4:6).

In Genesis chapter 30 verse 22, we read that God remembered Rachel

> "Then God remembered Rachel; he listened to her and opened her womb"

It is my prayer indeed that God will remember every reader of this book seeking the fruit of the womb in like manner in Jesus Name.

I had said in the earlier chapters that the fact that I have been using the term or that the Bible has been using the term 'and God remembered' does not mean that He actually forgot you or your circumstance. God cannot forget. God is too meticulous in all His dealings to forget anything especially His people. God is too organised, He is such a being that has done and likes everything done properly, and everything with Him is well sorted out! There is no way that He can forget you. He has aligned and arranged everything about you and for you before you were born, before you were formed as He said in the book of Jeremiah 1:5

> *"before you were formed in your mother's womb, I knew you and I have appointed you to be a prophet to the nations!"*

In the very same way, God knows you too; before you were born He already made plans and arrangements for you. The times you spend waiting for Him to do something for you and the fact that those things are yet to be done is an indication sometimes that the time for those things have not yet come. When the time comes, nothing can stop it as declared in Psalm 102 verse 13! Listen to God's response to those who think He has forgotten them:

> *"But Zion said, "The LORD has forsaken me, the Lord has forgotten me. Can a mother forget the baby at her breast and have no compassion on the child she has borne? Though she may forget, I will not forget you! See, I have engraved you on the palms of my hands; your walls are ever before me".* **Isaiah 49:14-16**

Man Is God's Image Of Remembrance

I remember an experience from my younger days, I didn't know why back then and I still don't understand why even now, but I could never get the correct answer in regard to the times table when asked for the answer of 9 x 5! (Strangely, I ended working in the mathematical field as an accountant!). Not that I was a dullard, I was actually very good with my times tables, I could reel out the '5' times tables 5 x 1, 5 x 2, 5 x 3 etc. I knew the answer to 5 x 9 and I would readily tell you the answer is 45 but if you swapped that round and asked for the answer of 9 x 5, it was a huge problem for me, I could never get it right! I honestly did not know why and I still don't know why that was the case.

I had a teacher back then, a certain Mr. Taiwo of blessed memory. He helped me get the right foundation for mathematics. With anything in life, the right foundation is very important. Before you marry anyone, it is important to find out about their foundation. Seek out the foundation of the home you are about to enter, indeed ask God for insight about any house you are about to move into because the wrong foundation could ruin you and could make life difficult for you (see Psalm11:3). Certain things you pray about might not be resolved if there is a problem with the foundation of the house you are living in spiritually.

Mr. Taiwo was such a strict disciplinarian who did not mess about with his responsibilities or his duties and you could not mess him about either. If you were hiding behind your mother, he will spot you out! Once I went to the market with my mother, she was in the meat market and we bumped into Mr. Taiwo who also happened to attend the same church as my family, he worked as an usher in the church. We met him in the meat market and after exchanging pleasantries with my mum, he said to me 'Tunde how are you?' I said 'fine thank you sir!' Then he said 'your tables please', so I recited the '5' tables, when I finished he said, 'your '9' tables please', I recited it until I got to 9 x 5 and I got stuck! Because of that experience, I worked hard to create a mental image of 9 x 5 = 45 in my mind so whenever I met Mr Taiwo and he asked for my '9' times tables, I would recite it and when I got to 9 x 5, I would refer to the image in mind!

Now, if I as a man could devise a way of remembering something, how much more the Almighty God that we serve, the All Knowing God. He says you have been engraved in the palm of His hands! That is His way of ensuring you are ever present in His mind. He can not forget you, I don't know what you have been going through, but it is guaranteed that the God of heaven will remember you! That womb of yours will carry a baby! I declare that your bank account will be swollen with funds and your health will be touched by the hand of God and your children shall walk in fear of the most High in Jesus Name!

As previously discussed, God will remember you when you take certain actions like the three men we have examined, certain things will not change for example, we can only receive from God when we pray, prayer will remain a constant because it is God's word. In **1Sam 1:10**, we see that Hannah prayed and after Elkanah her husband slept with her (Verse 19) God remembered her! She prayed before something happened!

Chapter 6

MORE BENEFITS OF REMEMBRANCE

Now let us turn our attention to more benefits or other gains that accrue to a person who has been remembered. In the scripture verses we have looked at, it says that the Lord declared 'I will remember', and in the book of Romans chapter 9:15b, God declares:

> *"I will have mercy on whom I will have mercy and will have compassion on whom I will have compassion".*

Dear child of God, please consider very carefully what I am saying to you, no one ever receives divine remembrance or divine visitation and have their lives remain the same; something positive always happens to any person who is remembered or has an encounter with the Most High God! There is always a forward movement in the lives of such people and the peace of God is also very evident in their lives. Whoever receives divine visitation from God always has some form of personal benefit from such a visitation. We see how Hannah, after her personal encounter with God, after that God visited her, became a mother, and not just any mother but she became the mother of the very first prophet in the Promised Land, the prophet called Samuel! We can mention a host of other people in the Bible including Abraham, Isaac and Jacob who became beneficiaries and recipients of many a physical blessing because God remembered them!

The Holy Spirit has made me to realise that being divinely remembered goes beyond just having a personal enjoyment or benefit of such a remembrance, there are other benefits that accrue when you are remembered and it is my earnest desire and prayer that everyone reading this book will be remembered of God as you open your ears and minds to listen to the heartbeat of God, He will liberate you in Jesus Name! I believe that the time for you to be remembered is here and now! Ps 102:13 states that now is the time, and today is the day, yes your time to be pardoned has come, your time of favour has come.

ACCUSERS WILL DISPERSE

God has shown me that one of the first things that happens when He remembers somebody, i.e. one of the gains that accrue to someone He has remembered; is that such a person's accusers will be dispersed and made non-existent!

Let this serve to give you joy, even when you are still in the valley, when you are yet to successfully make it to the mountain top, let the assurance that He will remember you and that His remembrance will bring about benefit to you, propel, encourage and energise you to get to the top.

The Lord has said that all your tormentors and accusers concerning that very thing that you trusting

Him for will go into extinction. As I look through the Bible, I find that everybody who faced opposition, all the children of God who went through difficult times at the hands of satan and his cohorts whether such attacks were on their marital lives, their finances or even their job roles/positions, God had a way of coming through for them such that their opposition have either disappeared or the Lord took their very life! I don't know what you are going through or what is bothering you now. It may be a boss or a manager in your office who is making life difficult for you but trust me when I say that when your time comes for God to remember you in that situation, all your opposition and all who oppose you will be made to disappear one way or another, you will not have to see or deal with them anymore!

Take your time to study the book of first Samuel, i.e. the entire book of first Samuel. Do you not realise that after the scripture says in the book of first Samuel 11:9 that

> *"and God remembered Hannah when her husband slept with her",*

Nothing further was heard of Elkanah her husband, nor of Peninah - her husband's wife! If perhaps you are suffering a similar fate or situation where some family members have said that you are not meeting up to family expectations and as such are causing trouble for you and seeking to destroy the love your husband has for you, I assure you and I decree that they will fade away in Jesus name! God has a way of doing these things.

In John chapter 8 and verse 1, a lady had been caught in adultery and the voice of her accusers was very loud, indeed the Bible says that this woman was caught red handed in the act! Some group of people took upon themselves the responsibility of being her accusers so that she may be stoned to death. They saw it as their job to ensure she received due punishment of death - such people never see the good side of anything or anyone. If you have such people around you, there is no need trying to fight them, because their job is to try and slow you down, try and prevent you from getting where you are going, you need to separate yourselves from them, ignore their antics and carry on in the hope and expectation that God will remember you!

Yes, this lady was caught in the act and yes she was guilty as charged however as they tossed her about and shoved her towards the place where they had planned to stone her and end her life, she stumbled in the direction of Jesus until her accusers stood in Jesus' presence. It just so happened that this was her day of remembrance, the day God had remembered her and her journey through life so far. Having stumbled into the path of Jesus, the accusers thought it was a great opportunity not just to stone this woman to death, but also to test Jesus' resolve and His obedience of the law! So they laid their accusations before Jesus and asked Him;

> *"what shall we do to her because according to the Law of Moses, she should be stoned to death!"* John 8:2

DESTINY RESTORED

The Bible records that Jesus appeared to ignore them, He simply bent down and wrote on the ground with his fingers. I believe based on the exposition of God's word to me that Jesus was writing the destiny of that woman.

I pray that your destiny will be written in the same way; it appeared that she was destined to die on that day however Jesus re-wrote her destiny! He who had the power of life and death (Mathew 28:18a) and the power over history re-wrote the history and thus the destiny of that woman! Not only was she not going to die on that day but Jesus caused all her accusers to disappear and fade away! Jesus answered her accusers with a very simple statement:

> *"he that sinneth not, let him cast the first stone!"John 8:7b*

And He went back to re-writing that lady's destiny.... Possibly writing things like 'I will bless you, you will live a long and fulfilled life, your family will prosper and people around you will make it' etc. by the time He arose from re-writing her destiny, the Bible records that all her accusers had one by one dropped their stones, their missiles and their instruments of destruction and disappeared unannounced! Do you know that for the rest of that Bible chapter and indeed for the rest of the entire Bible, none of those accusers were ever mentioned again! They seemed to have disappeared into thin air just like your accusers and all those who trouble you will soon become a thing of the past as the Lord remembers you in Jesus Name!

Perhaps what Jesus was writing on the ground in addition to rewriting this lady's destiny was the sin of the accusers, perhaps he was writing their names and beside their names he was listing the number of times they had committed adultery themselves and who they committed it with. You will find that a lot of the time, those who accuse you of something are guilty, or even more guilty of the same sin they accuse you of (see Luke 6:42). I can imagine that the leader of the gang of accusers had five wives at home and many other concubines. It is possible that God will simply expose your accusers and your detractors for who they are and they will fade away as a result because when light comes, darkness can not comprehend it or dwell with it!

YOUR ACCUSSERS WILL IMPLODE

Consider Pharaoh and how he would not let Israel go, even after he let them go, he changed his mind and pursued the Israelites even into the ocean as recorded in Exodus 14:9, it appeared Israel was doomed and Pharaoh was about to have his day but God turned things around and Israel came out victorious with no Egyptian in sight! I encourage you, when things around you look really bleak and it appears your enemies have the upper hand against you, don't worry and don't fret because God will remember you and bring you out, He will dispose of your enemies and you will come out victorious in Jesus Name. Exodus 14:28 tells us that the water flowed back over the chariots and the armies of Pharaoh and they all perished!

I decree that all those enemies who have decided that you will not make it, that they will not let you go from the bondage holding you down, that you will not enjoy your marriage, that you will not enjoy your life, that you will not enjoy your breakthrough in life, as the enemies of the children of Israel entered of their own accord perished into that Red sea and perished, so will your enemies perish in the Name of Jesus!

I am saying to you for definite child of God that there are accusers standing against you, enemies who want to ensure that you do not enjoy the best God has prepared for you however, God will remember you and you will enjoy life and enjoy the sight of the extinction of your enemies! They will become like a non-existent thing because you will see them and the work of their hands no more and you will be left to operate and enjoy God's goodness freely!

> *"Though you search for your enemies, you will not find them. Those who wage war against you will be as nothing at all".*
> Isaiah 41:12

There is a way God gets round situations in your life, if for instance you have a mother in-law who you consider to be bad and in truth she is a wicked woman, don't bother with fighting her in the physical and being mean to her in return, just go on your knees and ask God to remember you, and all your toil and all your prayers. I tell you, unless you are a paperweight Christian, things will become too hot for that mother in-law and she will by her own decision or by her own error leave you alone to enjoy your husband and your home! There is a way God gets round this kind of people, anyone who stands against you accusing and stopping you from enjoying your home and your marriage, God knows exactly what to do and how to deal with them!

I recall in the story of Daniel when other leaders, his colleagues got together and began to accuse him, they planned and schemed and had Daniel cast into that lion's den, the Bible records that first thing the following morning, the king rushed to the den and called out to Daniel:

> *"Has the God, whom you serve, been able to save you from the mouth of the lions?"*
> *Daniel 6:20b*

I declare to you that same God who delivered Daniel is able and will deliver you! Daniel answered the king and said:

> "Yes my king, the God whom I served sent His angels and shut the mouth of the lion!" Daniel 6:22a

In Daniel 6:24, we read that the king then made a decree commanding that every one who had accused Daniel be thrown into the lion's den and the accusers became the lion's breakfast. Their lies and schemes became their destruction!

What I have been trying to depict is that beyond having a personal benefit for being remembered of God, another gain of being remembered is that God will do away with your accusers and all those who oppose you and will not allow you to enjoy your life.

Such persons will simply disappear into 'oblivion', into a place where you will not know where they are. Don't be surprised if that boss who has been making things difficult for you suddenly fails to turn up for work, you will probably find out later that he or she has developed a sickness.

"It is the Sovereign LORD who helps me. Who is he that will condemn me? They will all wear out like a garment; the moths will eat them up". Isaiah 50:9

I remember once in a place where I used to work, there was a lady who constituted herself into a nuisance and a terror to everybody else in the office, she started to pick on me and to make things difficult for me because I had started a lunch time prayer meeting which was doing well. During one of our meetings, we got together and prayed against all such evil people. I got to work one day and I was told to sign a card, I asked 'what for?' They said 'oh, Ms X is sick and in hospital', I asked what had happened and they said, 'dont worry, we will tell you later'. I can tell you that the lady never returned to that office! Things like this are part of the benefits God gives to those who serve Him when He remembers them (see Psalm 35:1).

Chapter 7

YOUR PAST IS IMMATERIAL

Another benefit that accrues to believers when God remembers them is that the past becomes immaterial and irrelevant. Whatever it is you have done in the past ceases to matter and is no longer a factor in the equation of life. God is the kind of God who blesses you when your time to be remembered comes and it does not matter if the whole world is pointing an accusing finger against you at that point as recorded in Romans chapter 8 verse 31.

> *"What, then, shall we say in response to this? If God is for us, who can be against us?"*

Consider carefully what I am saying to you because sometimes we have mixed understanding of God's Word and bring emotions into the interpretation of the Word. God is a compassionate God but He dislikes unnecessary emotions when there are realities in front of us to be dealt with. When you cry for example because you have sinned, it does not impress God except you have repented or are crying in repentance.

I will say it again, when God remembers you, your past becomes irrelevant and I have no doubt about this because there are examples in the Bible. Let us take a look at someone in the Bible in the person of the apostle Paul. He was known as Saul before his conversion and on his Curriculum Vitae (CV), it was recorded that he breathed murderous threats against the church of God and indeed oversaw the execution of Stephen. Paul was an accuser of the brethren, an accuser of people in the faith, a persecutor and a murderer! He was well hated and disliked and indeed feared by those who served God because the Bible says right from when Saul featured from Acts chapter 7 to Acts chapter 9, verses 1 & 2, he was seen as a murderer. The children of God were so terrified of him that not one of them wanted any encounter with Saul of Tarsus!

Now the scripture says from Act 9:3-5 that Paul was on his way to Damascus to wreak havoc on the children of God. Verse 4 says

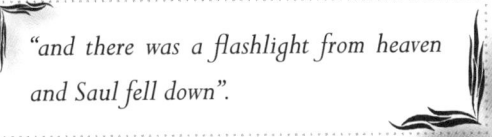

"and there was a flashlight from heaven and Saul fell down".

Now verse 5 says a voice from Heaven called out to him and said;

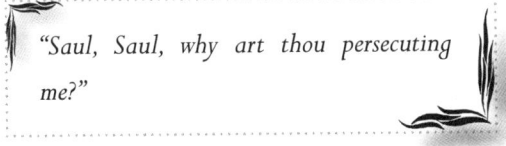

"Saul, Saul, why art thou persecuting me?"

Saul answered in the same verse;

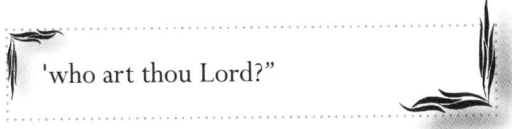

'who art thou Lord?"

This indicates to me something of interest. This is a man who never knew the Lord, indeed his whole existence was to wipe out the name of the Lord, and he never wanted to hear that name! But when God met? him on the way to Damascus, He introduced himself? by that very name Saul hated to hear, 'I am the Lord'. Now the thing of interest is this, when God called out to Saul, He did not originally introduce Himself, He simply called him 'Saul, Saul' and as recorded in Verse 5, Saul immediately answered, 'Who art thou, Lord'. Notice and check it out for yourself, that a capital 'L' was used here suggesting that Saul knew immediately that he was dealing with the Almighty and not just some a 'lords' in the house of Israel! I have personally looked at 7 or more versions of the Bible and each time, the capital 'L' was used in Saul's reply! So who told Paul that it was the Lord God Almighty who had called Him? How did he know the very person he hated and wanted nothing to do with, the very person or name He was trying to wipe of the face of the earth?

Let me pause here and say this, you may be in a situation in your work place or in any other setting where someone doesn't like you. They dislike the mention of your name so much that they have taken it on themselves to wipe out your name. Indeed sometimes, they refuse to call you or address you by your name, they choose to call you something else and simply speak to you or about you without using or mentioning your name. I say to you, do not worry, when the Lord remembers you, they will call you by the very name they hate and they will call you by your name with respect, with fear and with awe because you are a child of God!

CHANGE YOUR WAYS

I asked God once why He allowed such people to continue to exist, God explained to me that every one who is doing some form of evil or another knows what they are doing. They know they are being wicked. They know that they are persecuting you because your name is called Victoria or Elizabeth; because your name is Christ like. They know you have a spiritual background because you are called Benedicta 'a grace'. They know what they are doing and they say things like: 'Look at this person, who is this person who wants to give grace? Who is this Elizabeth, do you want to give birth to another John the Baptist? Who is this called Mary, do you want to give birth to another Jesus? They just want to hate you for nothing. God said they know what they are doing but I the Lord will always give them room for repentance. That is why Ezekiel 33:11 says that I the Lord do not want to see the death of a sinner but for him to repent.

In the book of Isaiah chapter 26 verses 10, God said:

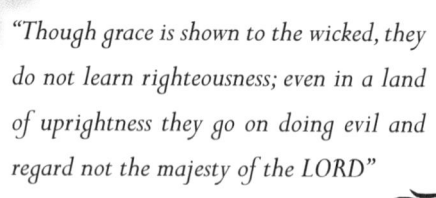

"Though grace is shown to the wicked, they do not learn righteousness; even in a land of uprightness they go on doing evil and regard not the majesty of the LORD"

Are you a wicked person? What spirit is in you? I want to say this to you, please child of God, whatever evil you are doing, drop it today. Some of us know that what we are doing is wrong and we have refused to stop, God is giving you the grace to repent today.

Paul had the grace to change which is why he knew that it was the Lord speaking. He is giving you grace according to Isaiah 26:10 which we just looked at. He said even the wicked will find grace. It was grace that Peter received that kept his position as a disciple. What Peter had done was enough for Christ to say bye-bye Peter, it's been nice knowing you. In Matthew chapter 26 verses 69-75, the Bible says that Peter wept bitterly after he had betrayed Jesus. He repented from the evil he had done. It was also grace that the prodigal son received because when he came to his senses, he said 'I will arise and go to my father' (Luke 15:17). I want you to arise from where you are and go to your father and say: 'Lord, I have sinned against you, please forgive me'.

GOD HAS THE POWER

We are still looking at the second reason why your past will be immaterial when God remembers you. But let's have a little Bible study in between. The second thing I noticed in this intriguing encounter raised the question; where was all this energy that Paul had? Some versions of the Bible say that he was breathing murderous threats, seething with active anger as he travelled to Damascus to wreak havoc on everyone who named the Name of the Lord. Immediately following Christ calling this young man and he heard the voice of Christ; the Bible says that he fell down (see Act 9:4).

So I asked God this question, I said with all this power that appeared to be in Paul and with him, what happened all of a sudden, where did all that power go? The Lord said to me, son, irrespective of what you are going through, and no matter how powerful your opposition may be; I have the power! It is immaterial what my children may be going through; I have power over all other powers. Paul's plan was to ensure that other Christians meet the same fate as Stephen, he intended to re-enact the stoning of Stephen in the lives of other believers; this is exactly what he was planning to do in Damascus. By the time he met with

Jesus Christ the possessor and maker of all power (1Chro 29:12), Saul became powerless. He lost all that murderous energy that was blowing within him.

Let me make a few prophetic declarations over your life: I am standing on the rock of Christ today, and I declare over your life that all the powers that are contesting with the power of God in your life will be dissolved the same way Saul's power was dissolved in Jesus Name. All such powers will be dissolved over your family at the command of your mouth just as hearing God's voice alone disarmed Saul.

So Saul was completely disarmed and he couldn't do anything, in addition to losing his strength, he became blind! I declare that your enemies will become blind to you and trouble you no more. Every enemy who says you are going to lose your job and those who say that they are going to uproot your marriage, the Lord will uproot them in Jesus Name.

The power we are talking about is the power of God Almighty, a God that possesses all the power in the heavens, in the earth and underneath the earth. Jer 32:17 declares

> *"Ah, Sovereign LORD, you have made the heavens and the earth by your great power and outstretched arm. Nothing is too hard for you".*

Rev 4:11 also states:

> *"thou art worthy to receive all the glory and power, for thou has created all things for they pleasure and thy power".*

Furthermore, Ps 65:5 buttresses the point:

> *"You formed the mountains by your power and armed yourself with mighty strength".*

This is the God I am talking about; He has the power over everything and over that situation, and that sickness that you are dealing with. It would take God less than a minute to dissolve the power of all those who have gathered to see your downfall. This is the God that I am talking about.

God told me clearly to say this to you as you read this book, He said: "Tell my people, that whatever the opposition that is facing them, I will forget their past and I will dissolve the power of the opposition" in the Name of Jesus.

UNDERSTAND TIMES AND SEASONS

The third thing? that I found about why your past becomes immaterial is this - Paul knew his time to be remembered had come! I encourage you to be like the sons of Issachar as recorded in the book of 1st Chronicles chapter 12; please learn to study the times, understand when you are doing something wrong, and know when you are going beyond your boundaries and caution yourself! Say to yourself: "I have got to be careful, I have stolen enough; I have lived a prayer-less life enough and I have to go back to God". Study times, situations and seasons and don't let sentiments override your good sense of judgement. Decide by yourself that you have fought against your parents wishes enough, they may be bad but realise they are still your parents.

There was a time I was praying with a certain person, and after praying nothing happened. Due to a revelation, I asked this fellow if he still had any surviving parents. He told me they were alive but asked what had that got to do with anything, he just wanted to leave that. I said that we can't leave that; they may be bad but they are your parents and you owe them certain responsibilities which you ought to fulfil, do what you are supposed to do for them. Don't say my parents are bad, they are evil therefore I owe them nothing (see Exodus 20:12). If you are abandoning your parents, you are abandoning yourself and when you have the oppor tunity through a book like this or during a one-to-one with a pastor or church brethren, take it that the right time to change has come.

Paul knew that definitely, his time to be favoured had come. How come this God will meet with me after all I had done? How come I was the one Christ came to meet and said do you know I am the one you are persecuting? Definitely this God must have seen the energy in me and that I am using my energy in a wrong manner and He wants it to be channelled into a good cause. Some of us use our energy and our strength against our wives and children. You beat and abuse your wives and children with reckless abandon, do you not realise that your strength is given to you as a man to protect and nurture your family? Instead you have taken that strength and used it wrongly.

Hear what the Spirit is saying to you today, re-channel your energy to something good, re-channel your power to something productive, Paul realised that he had been using his energy and his power wrongly, he must have thought to himself, 'I have been using this power to persecute and destroy innocent believers unjustly when I should have been channelling it for evangelism'. It must have been my time! He worked with his timing and didn't miss it and God heard him.

Children of God, hear what God is saying to you, despite everything Paul had done; he was the coroner who signed the death warrant or certificate of believers like Stephen (Act 8:1) yet God rendered all of that immaterial when he remembered Him. Perhaps situation and circumstances or maybe even stupidity and wrong counsel had caused you to enter into three previous marriages wrongly, but when the time comes for God to bless you, these mistakes will be irrelevant. In spite of all that Paul did to believers, I searched the entire Bible from Genesis to Revelation and realised that after Paul's encounter with God, God never again mentioned Paul's previous lifestyle or the many sins that he committed against God and His church. There is absolutely no record of it anywhere but only people like you and I, human beings remember it and make a record of it. When Paul tried to join up with the apostles after his salvation, they all refused to associate or be associated with him, indeed some still ran away at the sight of him until Barnabas took Paul and presented him formally to the Christians (see Act 9:27).

The Christians referred to Paul's past and always referred him to his past. I actually researched this fact and without a shadow of a doubt, God never referred to Paul's former way of life again anywhere in the Bible.

> "none of the sins he has committed will be remembered against him". Ezekiel 33:16

This is what the God we are dealing with has said. As soon as you declare that you are for God, none of the sins you have committed in the past will be remembered ever again. You may have performed innumerable abortions until your womb has been removed but when you say I have had enough and I am coming to you Lord, you will be surprised that you will be producing twins when your friend or your peer who was a virgin when she got married is struggling to have even one child! I know a true life story that illustrates this very point!

Chapter 8

TESTIMONY - AN IMMATERIAL PAST

There is this sister who was a virgin, had never been touched by a man until she married her husband, you can describe her as a brand new vehicle straight from the factory. There was another lady who had engaged in all manner of sexual devices and had destroyed her womb in the process. When she eventually got born again and started to serve God, people actually derided her and said after she had destroyed her life and her body sleeping with all manner of men, she was now claiming to be a Christian – deceiving her own self. Whenever a man showed an interest in marrying this second lady, on the advice of her pastor, she always told them her entire story before things had developed too far. She didn't want them to have any surprises or find out later down the line that she had lived a wayward life. Indeed she told them there was no way she could ever have a child because she had destroyed her womb. Almost all men disappeared as soon as she told them her story and never returned.

Eventually, a new manager was posted to the branch of the bank where she was working at the time, this manager saw this lady, she was hard working and always the first to arrive at work and the last to leave as well. He asked her once to take it easy and go home to spend time with her husband and children and she told him she was not married. It so turned out that this manager had recently been jilted by his long term girlfriend/fiancée. The man began to show an interest in the young lady and this time she went to her pastor and said, "all this while, you have told me to be open about my past, I am concerned that I will never get anyone to marry. Permit me not to tell my story to this man now showing an interest in me", but her pastor said "no, believe in God and believe the words that I say to you; (2 Chronicles 20:20) go and tell him all your story", so she did as her pastor had told her. When she tried to tell this manager (who had now proposed to her) about her past, she could not bring herself to say anything for fear of receiving the same treatment she had received from the other men in the past.

She explained her difficulty to her pastor so he asked her to get the man and for both of them to meet him in his office. On the day they came to see the pastor, he said to her yes sister so and so, you said you have something to say to brother so and so, please commence! She said to the man, I have lived a reckless life in the past, so reckless that my womb has been removed! The man said what? The pastor said well, it is as you have heard, do you still intend to continue with this relationship? The man said by the grace of God, yes! The pastor asked again, are you sure? He said yes! So a date was fixed and it turned out that there were two wedding ceremonies in the same church on the same day. The other lady getting married based on the testimony of the husband was a virgin! Within the first year of the marriages, the sister without a womb had given birth to her first set of twins meanwhile the other sister was still trusting God for her first child. In the second year of the marriages, the same sister without a womb had her second set of twins this time a set of boys, the first had been a set of girls yet the sister who married as a virgin was still trusting God! God had remembered the so called barren sister! Believe me when I say that when God remembers you, your past becomes immaterial!

ANOTHER TESTIMONY

I was on a missionary journey to Ghana sometime ago so as to tally with the rest of the story recently and after one of the meetings, a lady came up to me in tears and said everything you talked about today was about me! This was a very well organised ministry, I said it was not right for her to speak with me as there was a resident Pastor for her to speak with if she needs any further assistance, the resident Pastor prevailed that I should grant her the audience to speak with me and I took her to a corner of the church where we could talk. She said to me 'pastor, I misused my life!' she said she had slept around with every man in her life, she had slept with her sister's husbands and all other manner of men so much so that she had no friend, everyone had rejected her and turned their back on her! She had created all manner of discord amongst her friends and family as a result of her ways. Only one friend agreed to take her in as everyone rejected her and that friend brought her to the meeting where she met me. I counselled with her a bit and told her what needed to be done including the need for deliverance.

She sent me a text about a year later to say that she had found a man who wants to marry her, we want to fix a date and we would like you to be there she said in her text. She had also been without a job and was finding it difficult to secure a job because she could not obtain a reference from her previous place of employment as she had been sleeping with her boss and the wife of the boss got her sacked and had made it impossible for her to obtain a reference from the company! Whenever there was a request for a reference, it ended up on the desk of the wife of the owner of the company who always ensured no reference was provided. In her text to me, she said I am now gainfully employed with Ghana Airways and if you don't mind sir, I can help arrange a ticket for you on your next trip to Ghana!

This was a person who had misused her life, but when the time came for her to be remembered, her past did not matter! She now had a job and a husband in waiting! I had told her when she was speaking to me a year before that if she truly wanted to commit her life to God, she should renounce her sins (Psalm 66:18, Prov 28:13), get involved in the church, re-dedicate her life to God and get baptised into fellowship with God. (I had heard an announcement during the programme that there was an upcoming baptismal class). She had done just that and a year later, God had turned her life around. This is the nature of the God that we serve, when you truly repent, when the time comes for God to remember you, your past will have no bearing on your future!

Rahab The Harlot?

Consider Rahab in the Bible, she was described as a harlot! Not just a prostitute but a harlot! To call her a prostitute is to refine her profession a bit, just as calling such services 'an escort' in modern English but the Bible called her a harlot. All through scripture she was referred to as Rahab the harlot! However when the time came for God to remember her, all of Jericho was brought down but as **Joshua 6:7** puts it

"Only Rahab the harlot and her family and everyone in her house was saved".

As a digression let me mention here that it is important to choose the places you go! Everyone in the house of Rahab on that fateful day was saved! Choose the places you go carefully because they could either save you or destroy you! If you go to the house of the rich because of their money, be careful so that you do not become complicit in their ritualistic lifestyle that brought about their blood stained wealth! Rahab's past was forgotten, and when you too truly repent and turn to God, your past will be forgotten! Ezekiel 33:16 will apply to you.

> *"None of the sins he has committed will be remembered against him. He has done what is just and right; he will surely live".*

Chapter 9

YOUR COMMUNITY WILL BENEFIT

The third benefit I want to speak about is this (recall the first two are: your enemy will go to total extinction, and your past will be forgotten):

People around you will benefit from your remembrance. When you call yourself a true child of God and you say God blessed me, God remembered me and people around you are not blessed or benefit from it, your blessing is incomplete and that is probably not true remembrance! When a man is remembered and his life is not touching or blessing others, then his life is perhaps not truly remembered.

Even if you simply got married after waiting a while, it could be that that wedding is simply to bring about a blessing in the life of someone in the family. People around you who do not even like you or appreciate you should be so blessed and touched by your remembrance that they will say 'even though we do not like him, yet we are being blessed because of him so we thank God!' It was God's remembrance of Abraham that saved Lot!

> "So when God destroyed the cities of the plain, he remembered Abraham, and he brought Lot out of the catastrophe that overthrew the cities where Lot had lived."
> Gen 19:29

If people's lives are not being spared because of you I tell you, you have yet to enter the divine remembrance of God. If people's lives around you are not being bettered, then that is not the remembrance I am talking about. People around you must enjoy your remembrance, your position and the place where you are because it is brought about by grace and it should be a blessing to others around you.

> *"I will make you into a great nation and I will bless you; I will make your name great, and you will be a blessing".* Gen 12:2

If people around you are not benefiting as a result of your position, then do something to benefit them. Think of what you can do to benefit those around you. For example, those who have surviving parents should regularly and on a monthly basis support their parents financially and otherwise!

There are people who will take up a prayer if they ever heard that you are troubled by anything because of the benefit that you are to their lives. Look around you, examine your lives and see if you have been truly remembered. As the Lord remembered Noah, He will remember you; He knows where you are and what you are going through. The hair on your head he has numbered, He will remember you and this will be characterised by the blessings in your life.

Chapter 10

ONE GOOD TURN

So far, we have been looking at Divine Remembrance, what this means and what happens when one experiences it. We have then moved on from there and we looked at other gains and benefits that accrue when one is 'remembered' by God. So far, our discourse has been one-sided. As heaven focused people and candidates for the most flawless kingdom there will ever be – paradise, we can not afford to be one-sided.

Generally in every sphere of life, it is not a good thing, neither is it a wise thing for any man (referring to the male and female man) to focus on just one side of any issue. It is a very selfish thing to deal with any issue with a single angle or a single view of things, it is something only the carnally minded should do! As God's children who expect God's remembrance in our lives, we must learn to focus on the two sides of every story or the two sides of every issue. So as we conclude this volume, we would do the right thing and look at the other side of the coin when it comes to activating God's remembrance in our lives.

> *"Anyone who receives instruction in the word must share all good things with his instructor".* Galatians 6:6

Let me encourage you with this and bring you to the realisation that when you take counsel from somebody about any issue, be ever ready to share the benefit of that counsel with the one who gave you the counsel. Where the person who gave you the counsel is your pastor, your father or your mother and any benefit of the things they spoke to you about come in, it would not be right for you to ignore the one who gave you counsel. Don't say to yourself at those times "let me keep this to myself", it would be a sin. You are meant to share good things with your mentors; your instructors are your mentors as are your parents and your pastors.

The Bible encourages us in Galatians chapter 6 as above that you should share the good news of the counsel you receive with the one who gave you counsel. It is not just about sharing the material benefits of the counsel that you receive, I am speaking now about showing the proper respect and honour by sharing the news or progress about your particular circumstances with the one who has given you counsel about it! It is only fair because they have wept with you in the time of pain so when the time of joy comes, let them be there to rejoice with you, and don't deny them this.

> *Do not be deceived: God cannot be mocked. A man reaps what he sows. The one who sows to please his sinful nature, from that nature will reap destruction; the one who sows to please the Spirit, from the Spirit will reap eternal life. Let us not become weary in doing good, for at the proper time we will reap a harvest if we do not give up. Therefore, as we have opportunity, let us do good to all people, especially to those who belong to the family of believers.*
> Galatians 6:7-10

You know that? We live in a world where our goodness is regularly thrown back at us. We live in a world where we are regularly frustrated by the very people who are close to us. We live in a world where the children we have laboured to bring up abuse and turn their back on us and we feel so frustrated about it we sometime wish we never had a child but God is saying "Do not be weary in doing good" (Galatians 6:9). Some people change as a result of what they have experienced at the hands of people because they become weary and tired of doing the good they know how to do. I want to encourage you not to become weary, carry on doing what you are doing as if doing it for God. Therefore as you have opportunity, please continue to do good to all people especially those who belong to the family of believers (Galatians 6:10).

As I stated earlier, it would be very selfish and self centred of us to focus only on God remembering us. The Bible teaches us clearly that there are two sides to remembrance. God is looking for a man or woman in whose hands or in whose body He can bestow His glory. We will look quickly at what it takes for God to bestow that glory into our hands. I will show you a few things and you will decide whether one good turn truly deserves another. What I am alluding to is that it is not right for God alone to do the remembering, we too have got to remember God in our lives and by our actions so let us consider that subject title: 'One good turn as they say deserves another'.

BE APPRECIATIVE

Whenever we plant, we expect to reap. These days the word planting or giving is no longer in vogue. In the Christendom, we regularly use the word 'sowing'. We have used it so much that even our Muslim brothers know precisely what we mean when we use it. I was speaking to a couple of muslim acquaintances once and they said they sow towards charity causes in order to reap, they said they support hospitals and they were telling me that we all need to sow. I quickly asked them, is there anything like that in the Koran too? They said the word does not appear in the Koran per se but you know, it is a common slang; most of our friends are Christians so that is what they use. In fact look at this shirt I am wearing, a colleague of mine in the office bought it for me and he said "I am sowing this to your life". I said "that is good". At least we are infecting the muslim world as well with our lingo.

Whichever word you want to use, whether planting or giving or sowing, it is one and the same thing. When we plant; when we sow, we all expect returns, we all expect to reap. No matter whom you are, no matter the level you are operating in or the circle to which you belong. Whenever we give something, we should all expect a return. Whenever we do something we all expect something to come out of it, it is naturally the way we have been made. It is in your genealogical system that when you give you want something back. It is a natural thing that when you sow you want something to come out in return.

> "Those who sow in tears will reap with songs of joy. He who goes out weeping, carrying seed to sow, will return with songs of joy, carrying sheaves with him".
> Psalm 126:5-6

One of the rewards the sower is carrying is that sense of joy when he is reaping the plant; when he is reaping the harvest, joy that God has made his seed to germinate. God has made this seed he planted to bring forth. It is a natural expectation, even a simple and ordinary thank you is part of the harvest so don't withhold it. When something is done for you,

I am saying to you that it does not matter who that person is who has done it for you. Forget about his level, whether it is the Pope or whether he is a Bishop, courtesy demands that you say Oh Pope thank you for yesterday. Don't say he is doing his job, it should be a natural thing to say thank you. The 'thank you' you said is simply this, you are telling the planter who has given you something in the past a reward!

THANK YOU IS IN ORDER!

Imbibe the culture to always say thank you! When you give your tithes and your offering, even though you gave it here on earth, it is a way of saying thank you to God for His blessings. Even though God demanded that we give our tithe and offering (Mal 3:8-10), it is still one way of saying thank you to Him. That is why God the father has demanded it from us. You will still discover that when you do this, further doors and blessings will open up to you. As a way of appreciating you for being appreciative, God says "I will open the floodgates of heaven to you". So for any time you and I plant or sow, we expect something back and Jesus put that in better and greater perspective in the book of Luke chapter 17:11-19;

> *"Now on his way to Jerusalem, Jesus travelled along the border between Samaria and Galilee. As he was going into a village, ten men who had leprosy met him. They stood at a distance and called out in a loud voice, "Jesus, Master, have pity on us!" When he saw them, he said, "Go, show yourselves to the priests." And as they went, they were cleansed. One of them, when he saw he was healed, came back, praising God in a loud voice. He threw himself at Jesus' feet and thanked him—and he was a Samaritan. Jesus asked, "Were not all ten cleansed? Where are the other nine? Was no one found to return and give praise to God except this foreigner?" Then he said to him, "Rise and go; your faith has made you well."*

A common sense understanding of the above scripture tells you and me that Jesus was expecting to be thanked; He wanted to hear the words 'thank you'. That is why He asked, 'Were there not ten that were cleansed? How come only one came back to say thank you.' So don't assume, don't just presume and say don't worry he is my father, he is meant to pay my school fees.

Growing up as a child, if you don't say thank you when you receive your school fees or pocket money, you are in trouble with my father because he will tell you yes, it is my duty to pay your fees, fair enough but if you do not say thank you, you are in trouble. The kind of upbringing I had, after my father gave us our school fees you would see my mother kneeling down and saying thank you my husband in the traditional way. We too as children will appreciate our father in a similar manner saying thank you sir. Now I noticed quickly enough in those days that, if you say a little thank you when you received your school fees, I noticed that the pocket money you get from my father would be commensurate to the level of the thank you he receives from you. You see, he would react to the level of appreciation he got from us as his children.

There were times when I had received my school fees and said a simple thank you dad and stood there waiting for the pocket money, he would bring out an envelope, reduce the quantity of notes in the envelope and hand it to me but at other times, when I gave him proper African 'thank you' when I received my school fees, he would hand over the pre-prepared envelope with no deductions (see Proverb 27:11)!

So what I am saying to you child of God is that everybody wants a thank you, everyone wants to be appreciated. I say to every young one reading this book, do not assume that because your parents are responsible for you; that they brought you into the world that they must feed you. Yes they have to, and that is a safe assumption but you might only get the standard basic necessities of life from your parents if you are an ungrateful child. You can have basic food but there will be no ice cream or desert to go with it. However, when you know how to say thank you, your father is more likely to buy you a lolly after you have had your meal. There will be extras that will come with the basics when we show appreciation. Some of us are simply living and getting by on the barest minimum standard of living, there are no extras to add to the flavour of life because we do not know how to say thank you.

God in His mercy Himself wants you and I to show a bit of remembrance by saying thank you.

I stated earlier that God is looking for men and women in whose hands he can entrust His glory. God is looking for men and women who can reciprocate what He has done for them or what He is doing for them. How can this be done? How can God trust anyone?

I believe that you can convince God that you are truly a person with whom He can entrust some of His goodness. How can you and I convince the Eternal One in heaven that Father, you try me with this you will see continually what I am going to do? Well, there are three ways in which you and I can do things that will put us in a vantage position; a superior position where God at all times will place us right where we belong.

God said in Isaiah 49.15-16 that there is a slim possibility for a mother to forget the suckling child she bore but He states clearly that while this may be the case, He will never forget you for you are written in the palm of His hand. So what are the things you can do to ensure you are constantly remembered? What is expected of you by the God who will never forget you?

CONSTANTLY REMEMBER GOD'S GOODNESS

If you want God to remember you and bring you out of that predicament that you find yourself in at the moment, from that nasty seemingly unending situation you are at this present time, then you must constantly remember God's goodness over your life.

"Bless the Lord oh my soul, forget not all His benefits" Psalm 103:2

"Do not be deceived: God cannot be mocked. A man reaps what he sows". Galatians 6:7

For you to sow good things that will put you at the forefront of God's agenda; three things are expected of you. They are probably one and the same thing but in three different dimensions and the first of these is the need for you to constantly remember the goodness of God in your life.

> "*Remember how the LORD your God led you all the way in the desert these forty years, to humble you and to test you in order to know what was in your heart, whether or not you would keep his commands. He humbled you, causing you to hunger and then feeding you with manna, which neither you nor your fathers had known, to teach you that man does not live on bread alone but on every word that comes from the mouth of the LORD. Your clothes did not wear out and your feet did not swell during these forty years.*
> Deuteronomy 8:2-4

God said to Israel, 'Remember how the Lord your God led you out of Egypt'. From whatever perspective you want to look at it child of God, for anyone to lead you out of trouble either on a part time or full time basis or whatever, that person must have loved you. Anyone that leads you out from such a predicament is a person that has an interest in you. 'Remember how God led you from Egypt'. Egypt was a place where these people had been tried, tested, impoverished and exposed to so many evils. God by Himself through Moses went there to lead them out of that problem. The servant of the Lord who was writing these words i.e. Moses; was reminding the children of Israel of the goodness of God in their lives.

He was saying to them; please remember this thing that God has done for you. God's goodness to you and your children in leading you out of that place is a thing that should constantly be in your memory. You may have been left in that state of slavery permanently. Some of you reading this book may have still been in your predicament permanently but yet this God came and brought you out and connected you to your destiny and the helpers of your destiny. "Don't forget this kind of a thing". (see Psalm 71:20-22).

Moses said to Israel, think constantly about this and be thankful; he further reminded them in Deuteronomy 8:4 "Do you realise that your shoes, your garment never needed to be changed". Everything was growing with you constantly, none of your clothes wore out, and none of your clothes became dirty. Can you see that? Can you imagine that! They didn't need to shop for new clothes, God renewed their clothes miraculously, they never needed to wash, God dry cleaned their clothes automatically, and they were constantly enjoying these free blessings from God. No wonder He is a God they call 'Provider'. Let me encourage you by saying that no matter what it is that is lacking in your life, God is the Provider and He is able to meet that need.

For forty years, everyone in the company of the Israelites lived their lives without the need to change their clothes or wash their clothes, try to picture that! Some of us cannot wear a shirt twice before it is dry-cleaned; as soon as we sweat that is it, the shirt is going to the dry cleaners. Moses was saying to Israel; constantly remember these things that God has done for you and your children.

something more appropriate, I don't know what it is in your life that you think God has forgotten. All you need to do is to go back to the God that provides constantly.

The psalmist says in Psalm 23 that the Lord is my shepherd; I shall not be in want because he knows God can provide for people for 40 years with clothes not wearing out and with shoes not becoming too small for their feet. The Apostle Paul reiterated that in Philippians 4:19:

> *"And my God shall supply all my needs according to His riches in Christ Jesus.*

Second Corinthians 9:8 states:

> *"And God is able to make all grace abound to you, so that in all things at all times, having all that you need, you will abound in every good work".* Genesis Chapter 15:1.
>
> *"He said I am your shield and your great reward".*

Is there anything that you think that God cannot do? He is your great reward, He is your great provider and He is the one that can meet that need in your life. All you need to do is to remember Him constantly, remember His goodness constantly.

Chapter 11

IF IT'S WORKING, THANK GOD FOR IT

Don't overlook the fact that something is working for you regularly, you have to thank God for such things. People who want God to remember them need to recognise and remember the things that are working for them. If there is anything that is currently working for you, start thanking God for it beginning from today.

I received a call one Sunday morning as I was getting ready for the Sunday service. My phone rang and the person on the other end of the phone was breathing heavily. She said Pastor, please I want you to pray for somebody I just met, let me give the phone to the guy. She passed the phone to the man who started by saying apologies Pastor for troubling you this morning, your church member met me here at the bus stop and we got talking, she was of the opinion that something was wrong with me mentally but I am absolutely fine. I simply have a heavy burden in my heart and it is troubling me. He agreed to meet with me that very morning and what he said to me is worth sharing here.

This young man who I estimate to be about 28 years old says he has been living in the London area since he was about four years old. He said that he and his family had been going to a church in the West London area and for some strange reason; some members of the church ganged up against the pastor and started to stir up all kinds of trouble within the church. Eventually, the church closed down as a result and he said 'this is where I have been getting my joy'. I never recognised the importance of the church until it was closed down and this is why I was at the bus stop on the Sunday morning with your church member, I was so confused as I didn't know where to go or what to do and the sister thought I had lost my mind! He said 'when I was standing at the bus stop, I suddenly realised I should've been in church but for the events that led to its closure - a church I have attended for over 20 years plus. All my friends were in the church, I have laboured there, I was about to be made the youth pastor and so on and so forth and some people caused this church to close down. I didn't know when I rushed to your sister and said "What is happening, can someone explain to me?'

The minute he said that, I tried to calm him down. I said "don't worry God is able; God will help you deal with the situation". After he left, the Holy Ghost asked me 'do you thank God that when you wake up on Sunday you have a church to go to?' This man had told me how the church services fitted appropriately into his Sunday schedule, he said he has been finding it difficult to locate another church to attend because he has been to 3 or 4 churches but found it difficult to settle there because he has to work on Sunday afternoon, the 9am — 11am services of his long term church suited him just fine!

After he left me, I began to meditate on these things, there are things that work well for us but do we thank God for them? Do you thank God for your child's admission? Do you thank God for going into your car, cranking the engine and the engine revs to life? Do you thank God for your wife?

DON'T TAKE THINGS FOR GRANTED

Recently, I was at the gym and another Pastor started up a conversation about the spate of immorality in the church of God. We talked about the number of pastors and ministers of God who have been involved in some sex scandal or another. Eventually we concentrated on the question of divorce amongst ministers of God and by the end of the discussion my heart was heavy for the church of God and I got dressed to leave the gym.

He said do you know what pastor? He said "I have never thought of it in my life that my wife can leave me. I have never actually prayed and thanked God for my wife and for the fact that I am married". I said "well, now you have grounds to be thankful". I said "you know what I am going somewhere now, I want to go and pray for somebody please accompany me". He accompanied me to the house of one of our members and after we prayed for them, they too raised the topic of a popular pastor's divorce. So we just prayed that God would intervene as soon as possible. When I dropped off the pastor who had accompanied me, I was alone in the car as I drove home and I said "God I thank you for my wife. I thank you for the most beautiful woman you ever made and gave to me as a wife".

If she says she is going to run away now or leave me now, what would I do? Back in the day, when she would say in anger that she will run away I would answer her and say no problem, I am not stopping you from leaving but as you are leaving, I will be right behind you with my own bags, wherever you go, I will go too! I had never considered the need to thank God for being a married person. Let me stress the point again, anything that is working for you, God wants you to appreciate Him for it. God wants you to constantly remember those things and be thankful for them. It is a mistake on our part when we do not thank God for the things that are working in our lives.

We should be thankful for the fact that we are still alive and well and breathing. We should thank God for life because we can never tell what tomorrow holds for us. God wants us to constantly thank Him for everything that is working for us. Don't overlook His goodness. If you want God to remember you, then stay grateful! As a saying goes "A man's favourite attitude should be gratitude". You are probably complaining that you have been married for the last five years with no babies but consider this: What about people that have never been married? People who have never known the joy of being in that blissful union? You are with your husband or your wife yet you are complaining instead of being thankful. When you have been waiting on God, remain in the state of thankfulness and you never can tell what God can do. He who forgets the language of gratitude can never be on speaking terms with happiness. Quit complaining, thank God for your situation and thank God for the bits that are working for you.

I am excited every Sunday morning when I wake up as I look forward to the service. I had taken it for granted that I have a church to come to every Sunday until I met with that brother. I am telling you the absolute truth when I say I had never taken the time to thank God for my church, never thanked God that I have a church to come to; I never appreciated this until that man sat in front of me with tears in his eyes lamenting the loss of his church. I said to myself after that, "This sends a message, a clear message." Appreciate God for what is working. Appreciate God for that job you still have to go to. Don't complain and say that you want to leave the job because people in the organisation are bad. You would struggle to pay your bills if you simply leave, nobody will pay your bills for you. Thank God instead for being there; at least you have a job that you can go to. May God grant us the grace to be thankful in Jesus' Name.

Chapter 12

REMEMBER WHAT GOD HAS DONE FOR YOU

"When you have eaten and are satisfied, praise the LORD your God for the good land he has given you. Be careful that you do not forget the LORD your God, failing to observe his commands, his laws and his decrees that I am giving you this day. Otherwise, when you eat and are satisfied, when you build fine houses and settle down, and when your herds and flocks grow large and your silver and gold increase and all you have is multiplied, then your heart will become proud and you will forget the LORD your God, who brought you out of Egypt, out of the land of slavery". Deuteronomy 8:10-14

In addition to remembering and thanking God for what is currently working for you, I encourage you also to remember the past good deeds of God.

Many of us are too need conscious and this is something that God really hates. People who are always need conscious focus on what they want and nothing else, nothing else matters in their relationships besides the thing that the want or need to have. Even when you meet their needs presently, they will return in the future with further demands with no regard for the relationship or the fact that their needs had been satisfied in the past.

This sort of a relationship is the worst form of relationship you can have with God and with man. If you are need conscious and focus only on what you are after then you will find it hard to remember God except when you want or need something from Him. Remember what God has done for you in the past, don't say after you have made it that you achieved it by your own power; don't let your success go to your head to the point where you forget about Him and everything he has done for you.

The Holy Spirit ministered to me some time ago that some people are still walking around the same mountain; going round in circles because they fail to acknowledge the fact that it is God who has actually kept them alive. Their focus has been more about what they want now, they want to get rich now, they want to get married now, and they want their job now! God told me to tell you that if this is your focus you will not be remembered.

If you are complaining that your wife is yet to give you a baby, what about your mates who do not even have a girlfriend much less a future partner to marry and these were perhaps your groomsmen at your wedding several years ago? You must learn to thank God and trust God by remembering the good times when God match-made you with your husband or wife. If you fail to remember the good things God has done for you in the past, you will experience further delay. Child of God, what do you think hindered. Israel's journey of

40 days to a 40 year journey? It was Israel's failure to remember the goodness of God that brought them out of Egypt with as much gold as they could carry!

FORGET HIS GOODNESS AND PAY THE PRICE

Let me take you through the story of Israel's exodus from Egypt once again as recorded in the book of Exodus chapter 3. Israel prayed the same kind of prayer that you and I pray today when we find ourselves in sticky situations. They cried out to God and said 'God, we have been in trouble for over four hundred years now, please save us from this slavery!' God heard their prayer and in the book of Exodus chapter 15 God brought them out. Do you know what? I struggled to find a proper record of appreciation from the children of Israel recognising that yesterday, or two days ago we were in slavery but God has now delivered us.

Thank God for Miriam who composed that song of thanksgiving 'there is none holy as the Lord, there is none besides Him, neither is there any rock like our God, there is none Holy as the Lord'. The Bible said that other women joined Miriam and they sang her song of praise but the men apparently did not join in. This is the only record we have of Israel's women appreciating God for what He had done for them. If failing to appreciate God was not bad enough, in Exodus 16 in the middle of the desert they got hungry and what did they do? The men went up to Moses, God's representative and gave him an ultimatum – they gave an ultimatum to the very one who had brought them out of Egypt with a mighty arm, they forgot very quickly what God had done for them.

A God who had brought them all the way including making a way in the sea and destroying Pharaoh's pursuing army; you would expect that they would trust him to give them food? Instead they went to the man Moses and said 'Listen up, we know you are an anointed man of God and we respect you because of your calling. By tomorrow if we do not have rice and beans with nice chicken on it you will see what we will do to you! We were living our lives quietly in Egypt with all kinds of vegetables before you caused all the trouble that made us to become exiles here in the desert. Who told you we were not happy in Egypt? If there is no food tomorrow Moses, you are in serious trouble!" My mother used to tell me to be grateful for what I have, not regretful for what I do not have. You can imagine how regretful this people were for what they do not have!

The Bible records in the book of Numbers chapter 20 verse 6

> *"Moses and Aaron went from the assembly to the entrance to the Tent of Meeting and fell facedown"*

I beg of you, please don't put your leaders through hard and difficult times because of your obstinate and ungrateful nature. As I was reading through Numbers chapter 20, I could understand fully what Moses and Aaron were going through and what they went to do inside the tent, I am sure they went there, fell face down before the presence of the Lord and wept! They must have said to God – would you let this people beat us up? Look at this people whom You have brought out of slavery, we expected they would be happy and thankful but instead they want to beat us up because there is no garlic and onions!

The Lord said 'Don't worry; I will definitely do something about it'. God rained down manna direct from heaven, He gave clear instructions about what they should do with the manna and they still disobeyed that and took too much! No one had ever eaten such food before, food directly prepared by God Himself! These obstinate people who enjoyed such benefit made my Lord and my God a cook and God willingly gave them cooked food from heaven. Was there a record that they said thank you? No! No thank you for bringing us out of Egypt yesterday and no thank you for the food of yesterday. No record of thank you.

And if this was not enough from the Israelites, they went back to Moses and pressed him even further with threats: Now we know that yesterday you gave us food from heaven but have you ever eaten without drinking water before? Have you? We are warning you again, we are serving you notice again that you must provide us with water or else we are going to drink your blood. Again Moses went and fell face down before the Lord and again the Lord said to him, don't worry simply 'go, strike the rock, water will come out'. Moses did as God directed and water came out of the rock right before their very eyes, they drank and were satisfied. Was there a record that they said thank you? No, none whatsoever.

After all this, The Lord told Moses to come up to the mountain top to meet with Him. Perhaps these people are misbehaving because they have no rules that guide them, come up and let me give you the rules and regulations to guide their behaviour henceforth. The man Moses went up for 40 days, meanwhile food was there for them to eat, clear spring water was gushing out of the rock for them in full supply - not chemically treated water but fresh water from the fountain of the earth. Water so fresh that if you bathed in it, and you had any skin disease such as eczema, all the eczema would disappear. It was water that would make your skin so smooth that you would lose any wrinkles on your skin.

Moses looked around him and said, of course Lord, I am on my way. There can't be any problem leaving this lot on their own – they have food and water, what else could they possibly want? What else could possibly go wrong?

> *"But if we have food and clothing, we will be content with that".* 1 Timothy 6:8

So Moses said, let them enjoy their food and water and I will come up to the mountain top! So Moses met with the Lord for forty days to pick up the Ten Commandments. Before he came down from the mountain top as recorded in the book of Numbers chapter 14 what happened? This ungrateful people had decided to name an image as their god who brought them out of Egypt! Moses came down to see Israel in typical idol worship! They had made an image of a calf and they started worshipping this image.

Moses thought to himself, even when God did all those miracles for these people, they did not dance much less sweat like this, now looking at them sweating in idol worship. Moses got so angry and wham! He slammed the tablets of stone upon which God had written the Ten Commandments, he broke them. Then God considered these acts of Israel, he looked at their sins and He said every one of this people who is over 20 years of age will not make it to the Promised Land, I will make them to go round and round and round until every one of them has died! And so a 40 day journey became a 40 year journey because Israel failed to keep in mind, to constantly remember the past and all that God had done for them.

Do Not Focus On Your Need

Forgetting the goodness of God is often times a direct result of being too need conscious. By need conscious I mean focussing too much on your needs that you lose sight of other relevant issues. If you are need conscious, you are very likely to forget the good things the Lord has done for you in the past.

> *"Therefore do not worry and be anxious, saying, What are we going to have to eat? or, What are we going to have to drink? or, What are we going to have to wear? For the Gentiles (heathen) wish for and crave and diligently seek all these things, and your heavenly Father knows well that you need them all. But seek (aim at and strive after) first of all His kingdom and His righteousness (His way of doing and being right), and then all these things taken together will be given you besides. So do not worry or be anxious about tomorrow, for tomorrow will have worries and anxieties of its own. Sufficient for each day is its own trouble".*
> Matthew 6:31-34 (AMP)

Take no thought for what you will eat or drink is the instruction from the Bible; live each day as they come and trust God to meet your needs. That is why one of the wisest men in the Bible besides Jesus said this:

> "Two things have I asked of You [O Lord]; deny them not to me before I die: Remove far from me falsehood and lies; give me neither poverty nor riches; feed me with the food that is needful for me, Lest I be full and deny You and say, Who is the Lord? Or lest I be poor and steal, and so profane the name of my God".
> Proverbs 30:7-9 (AMP)

He said two things I require from the Lord not to give me poverty or riches so that I will not forget Him. Don't be too need conscious; you want to pay your mortgage tomorrow, nothing else matters right now. You have to finish the school homework of your children and that is all that matters right now; such an attitude and outlook to life is not good.

Remember to thank God regularly for everything, both great and small. I came to this conclusion a long time ago that when I am overwhelmed by anything, I just sit back, relax, speak in tongues and thank God. Being need conscious is affecting and doing damage to many homes... you hear women saying 'my husband does not love me anymore', he is not a loving husband, but have you considered what he might be going through right now? Is it possible there is a reason why he is not expressing the love and affection that you crave? Think back to the times when he was a loving person; think back at the times when he had just met you. I am sure if he was a hateful person you would not have married him so there must have been a time when he was very caring and loving, don't focus on your need, explore other possibilities! The person who is all wrapped up in himself is overdressed, if a man is self-centred, he is off-centred.

Remember the days when things were fantastic between the two of you and consider the fact that the way your husband is acting now is not usual for your husband. Enquire about his job, what is going on in the office? What about the finances; is everything ok in the bank account? Look at the bank statements. Probably he is running on overdraft, you may find that there is something actually affecting his demonstration of love towards you. Stop focussing only on things that are happening right now, don't be totally now and need conscious.

Remember the past, count your blessings and name them one by one! Constantly think of the things the Lord has done for you in the past and when you do this, God will be happy with you. He will consider you and your acts of remembrance; He will appreciate the fact that you are thankful for the wife He has given you. He will appreciate the fact that you are grateful for the day you met your wife. God will appreciate the fact that you are grateful for your job even before you receive your first salary. God will respond by dealing with your issues with God speed that will keep you in the forefront of God's agenda.

God loved David extravagantly because he always remembered the past workings of God in his life. Before he faced Goliath, he recounted and recalled how the Lord had delivered him from the bear and the lion! I encourage you to make it a habit to remember the past goodness of God in your lives and when you do that, I am convinced that your case will ever be before the Lord.

❦

Chapter 13

SEEK GOD FOREVER

The third and final thing I want to encourage you to do besides being thankful for everything that works in your life and remembering every good deed God has done for you in the past, is to seek God eternally. No matter what you are going through or where you find yourself, let God know that He is your God. I was listening to the testimony of one of the deacons in our church recently, he had an issue with his job and he was saying during his testimony that even if he lost his job or had to walk away from it, God is still God! He said 'If this job or anything else is taken from him, would that make God to cease to be God?

What am I saying to you child of God is that you must let God know that God, you are my God, I will seek you forever, I will serve you forever and I will serve or know no other God. You are my God.

When you are constantly seeking God, you are in a sense constantly remembering Him. John chapter 15 verse 5 states that:

> "I am the vine; you are the branches. If a man remains in me and I in him, he will bear much fruit; apart from me you can do nothing".

If you want to bear fruit and if you want God to remember you, you must necessarily stay by Him, you must say to Him that God I am for you and I am part of you. Irrespective of anything that happens, I am for you. When you do things like that, you demonstrate to God that you are a part of Him, a part of his household.

Even God Himself said 'apart from me you can do nothing'… consider the scripture we just read, remain in God and He will remain in you. Let Him know constantly that He is the one you are seeking.

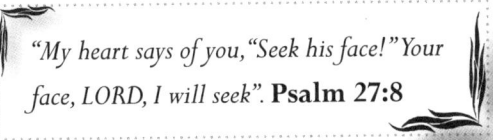

"My heart says of you, "Seek his face!" Your face, LORD, I will seek". **Psalm 27:8**

Are you seeking the face of God? Can it be said that even though you received a letter of termination you still said God you are still God, I will yet seek You; You are the one I am going to seek. "Whether it is favorable or unfavorable, we will obey the LORD our God, to whom we are sending you, so that it will go well with us, for we will obey the LORD our God." Jeremiah 42:6

Conclusion

Beloved as I conclude this volume, I want to encourage you as a child of God that it is very easy for God to remember you. All you need to do as His child is to make sure at all times that you thank Him for what is working, ensure you remember His past goodness in your life.

Thank Him for anything that is working in your life. Thank Him for your marriage, even though it is going through turbulence, yet be thankful and grateful. God may have given the instruction and it is the will of God that all should go and multiply yet not everybody will get married. Not everybody will give birth to children and the fact that you are privileged to be one of those who get married or have a child is something you should be thankful for.

Why should you forget the past goodness of God in your life because of what you are going through now? Why would you stop seeking Him? Be encouraged to seek God's face and His remembrance. One good turn they say deserves another. I am convinced that God has blessed you in some way or another, no one reading this book can honestly say that they have not received the grace of God in some measure. The fact that you are alive and have the ability to read this book is testament to the goodness of God in your life. You need to thank God for this grace, you need to appreciate Him for His goodness constantly and He will constantly remember you.